CW01647248

8 MAY 2

To JD.

THE DAY THE WORLD CHANGED.

WITH THANKS.

AS EVER

TCT

For the Fly-Leaf of an Anthology...

There is a garden where
  I have spent hours.
Would you like to go there,
  You, who love flowers?

There's a little blue* door
  Leads me to my garden.
I'll show you - and be sure
  You'll find it open!

In it's enchanted ground
  I think that you
May find flowers that I have found,
  And love them too.

Won't you go in, and look,
  Where I spend hours?
The door is this blue* book;
  Poems are the flowers.

Air Commodore Sir Henry Nigel St.Valery Norman Bt. RAF
1897-1943

*in Sir Nigel Norman's original poem the colour was green to match the cover of his *Verses 1911-1943*. The author has taken the liberty of changing the colour to blue in order to match the cover of this book.

Give Me The Wings

Give Me The Wings

A Celebration of English Aviation Poetry

With Some Other Aviation Writings

Selected and edited by
Martin Barraclough

"Give me the wings, magician, or I die."
The First Airman, Humbert Wolfe

WORDS by DESIGN

First published 2012 by

WORDS by DESIGN

www.wordsbydesign.co.uk

ISBN: 978-1-909075-02-3

The author with Francis Derwent Wood's statue of Daedalus preparing Icarus for the flight Bristol City Museum
(Author's photograph)

Dedication

Aerial bombing with 'dumb', that is unguided, bombs remains controversial to this day because of the huge collateral damage that it inflicts on the civilian population. This controversy has caused the delay of over half a century to the construction of the national memorial to the men of Royal Air Force Bomber Command that is being unveiled by Her Majesty Queen Elizabeth II in London's Green Park during the summer of 2012.

It is to the memory of those 55,573 young men who lost their lives during World War II that I dedicate this anthology.

Martin Barraclough
May, 2012

Contents

THE FIRST WORLD WAR: 1914-1918

THE GOLDEN AGE: 1918-1939

Foreword

I feel honoured and daunted to have been asked by my friend and fellow pilot, Martin Barraclough, to write the foreword to his remarkable anthology of aviation poetry. Martin is himself an accomplished author and poet, as well as a fine and adventurous aviator. He has also brought scholarship and meticulous research to what is obviously a labour of love; the result is something very special.

In my experience most anthologies of poetry are simply that – a carefully chosen collection of verse. Martin has gone much further. In his commentary he gives context to each piece, which greatly enhances the reader's enjoyment and understanding, while the lavish illustrations contribute further to the reader's appreciation.

Poetry is such a concentrated form of literature that it poses, I believe, particularly demanding challenges to the reader, as well as to the writer. Because of the richness and compression of its form, it is also a wonderful medium for conveying the intensity of feeling and emotion engendered by the experience of flight, especially for the pilot. It is significant, I think, that almost half the poems in this collection have been written by pilots. Because of the insights that Martin has provided in his thoughtful and well-informed introductions to each section and to individual poems, aviators who are not regular readers of poetry will find that getting the most out of a poem is greatly facilitated, and poetry lovers who know little of flying will savour the verses all the more for the background that Martin provides. And underlying it all, thanks to the time line provided by the way the poems are arranged, is a brief and attractively presented history of aviation.

Aviation poetry has a few great themes; the beauty of creation when viewed from the vantage point of the sky; mysticism and religion; freedom of movement and spirit that is hard to find elsewhere; and death. Death is the more prominent because the age of aviation has spanned two world wars and many other conflicts, and aircraft have turned out to be such a potent means of waging war. Thus much of the poetry – and in my opinion some of the best poetry – in this anthology is unavoidably not only aviation poetry but also war poetry, with themes of courage, sorrow and loss. That is right. Martin has ensured that everything is covered.

Martin tells me that his intention was to produce something quintessentially English; I think that he has succeeded, while still admitting some fine poems of other origins. His is the first English anthology of aviation poetry since *Wings, an Anthology of Flight* by HG Bryden, was published in 1942. It is therefore long overdue.

There are many previously undiscovered joys to be found between the pages of this anthology and much to be learnt from Martin's thoughtful introductions. It is also the kind of book that lives, rather than dies, on one's shelf. It is a book of manifold parts, a book to keep returning to, and in doing so to rekindle pleasures already discovered and to find new insights. I am sure that readers will treasure it.

Air Chief Marshal Sir John Allison, KCB CBE FRAeS RAF

Preface

In his preface to the 1802 edition of *Lyrical Ballads* William Wordsworth wrote "For all good poetry is the spontaneous overflow of powerful feelings: but though this be true, poems to which any value can be attached, were never produced on any variety of subjects but by a man, who being possessed of more than usual organic sensibility, had also thought long and deeply".

Flying an aeroplane requires plenty of 'organic sensibility' and because flying is of relatively short duration, there is much time on the ground to think 'long and deeply'. Although there is evidence of pilots reading a book while piloting their aircraft -- which can only have taken place on boring long distance flights -- I cannot believe that any serious poetry was written while hands were occupied with stick and throttle and the brain with the many changing circumstances of flying. Magee wrote to his parents that his famous sonnet *High Flight* 'started at 30,000 feet and was finished soon after I landed'. As he was flying a Spitfire on active service at the time, I think there is considerable poetic licence in this remark!

I have always been told that one of the first things that potential readers will do when picking up a book whose contents concern them is to go straight to the index to see whether they are mentioned – such is our vanity. In the same way, a person picking up an anthology will understandably look to see whether his or her favourite poem has been included; if not, there is immediate disappointment and a grave risk that the anthology is, without further inspection, deemed a failure. By this criterion I know that I will have failed a great many potential readers and not a few friends to whom I can only offer my apologies. In an endeavour to placate them and persuade them still to buy this collection I have added several blank pages to the end of the book to which I hope that they will attach their own favourite poetry and, indeed, their own work.

So what have been my own criteria for selecting the poetry for this offering? I have flown light aircraft for fifty-nine years, never militarily nor professionally, and mostly for enjoyment. I hope to continue to do so for a few more years while my faculties can still cope with the never-ending changes in regulation to which this pastime is subjected. I am still enthralled by the whole art of powered flight and the beauty of the environment in which this art is performed, an environment over which Man has no control and which is ever-changing, from the pure beauty of a cloudless blue sky to the mortal danger of embedded thunderstorms, requiring the pilot to exercise judgement and skill on every flight. Using the richness of the English language and the metre of verse, the poet, like the artist, is able to capture all the variety of this world of aviation, not only to commit to writing his own aspirations and experiences, but to inspire others who read that poetry.

I have tried to include as much poetry as possible that has been written by pilots themselves but have only achieved a fifty per cent success rate. Equally, I have tried to be very selective in my choice of War Poetry. So much poetry was written during both World Wars and most of it, understandably, dwelled on the grimness of war and life during wartime; it is well documented in the many books and anthologies that have been written during the last century.

Much doggerel has also been compiled, some of it bawdy, which was usually sung and forcefully enjoyed by high spirited aircrew as a means of releasing the awful tension of war-time operations and the constant apprehension that life expectancy for them was agonisingly short. With two exceptions I have left these to the many well thumbed song-books that exist and have been handed down by those who survived those dreadful times.

On the subject of doggerel, my constant companion, *The Oxford English Reference Dictionary*, simply defines doggerel as ‘poor or trivial verse’. *Chambers Twentieth Century Dictionary* is more pithy, calling it 'irregular measures in burlesque poetry, so named in contempt: worthless verse', while the more august *Shorter Oxford English Dictionary* has a similar description adding the adjective 'pedestrian'. *Collins Concise English Dictionary* calls it 'comic verse'. While I have labelled some poems doggerel I am happy to leave the reader to be the judge as to whether these and others deserve this title or not.

Although I am not an admirer of free verse there are several examples throughout the anthology. As with the prose that I have selected they contain sufficient of Wordsworth's 'powerful feelings' to warrant inclusion.

I am conscious that my sub-title refers to 'English Poetry' but that I have included poems and writings by Australian, American, French and Argentinian authors. These writings were too good to omit and they are, after all, in English!

I have chosen to place the poems in the chronological order in which they were written rather than by theme, but if it was more appropriate I have placed them chronologically according to the date of the event which they record. So, for instance, I have placed Foxley-Norris's *Envoi: Battle of Britain Pilot* in 1940 and not when he wrote it after the war.

I hope that I have re-discovered for the reader some long forgotten poetry, such as the work of Dorothy M Haward, Jeffery Day, and Paul Bewsher, and that readers will enjoy some that has never yet been published, such as the poetry of Prunella Power. My only sadness is that I will inevitably have omitted some good poetry; if readers will be kind enough to send such omissions to me I would love to read them and I too can add them to my own blank pages.

MCB
May, 2012

Prophecies and Aspirations 400BC-1903

Bust of Leonardo da Vinci at the entrance to the Italian Air Force Museum at Vigna di Valle
(Author's photograph)

Introduction

Una volta che avrai volato camminarai in terra con gli occhi rivolti verso il cielo perche' li' sei stato e li agogno a tornare.

Once you have experienced flying you will walk on earth with your eyes turned skyward because there you have been and there you will wish to return.

Leonardo da Vinci, 1452-1519

Man has always envied the birds and aspired to fly, believing, until little more than a century ago, that the only way this could be done would be by making for himself wings that were similar to those of a bird. Even after the Wright Brothers proved, in 1903, that flight in a heavier-than-air machine was possible, men continued to experiment with man-made wings, using only muscle-power, inevitably with disastrous – usually fatal – results.

There were many writings about Icarus, son of master craftsman Daedalus who, according to Greek mythology, escaped from Crete on wings made by his father of wax and feathers. Ignoring his father's warnings, Icarus flew too close to the sun which melted the wax and he plunged to his death.

The story of Icarus epitomised the hubris of youth and fitted exactly the popular conception of the pioneer aviators and their many disasters. It seems also to have imbued the modern-day journalist with the concept that all aircraft crashes are the result of aircraft 'plunging' from the sky!

Early flights in the late 1800s were made in balloons and gliders. Balloons, being lighter than air, but lacking in directional control, were able to lift people into the sky, mainly to enjoy the view or spot on the enemy, but never had the ability to travel effectively in a required direction, being at the mercy of the prevailing wind.

The poems in this short section not only reflect the bird's eye view of the world and the belief that the best medium for travelling the world will be the air but warn ominously of the extension of warfare into the sky.

Euripides, c480-406BC

A Chorus (from Iphigenia in Tauris)
Euripides

The earliest reference to Man's aspirations to fly that I could find was this extract from Euripides' epic play about the princess Iphigenia, daughter of Agamemnon. Written between 414 and 412 BC it is worthy of inclusion in any anthology. Sadly neither de la Bere, who included it in his *Icarus – An Anthology of the Poetry of Flight* in 1939, nor I, through the good offices of the world-wide web, could find the name of the translator of this extract.

Oh! Might I travel through yon lucid road,
Where rolls the chariot of the fiery God;
Might I through th' impassive air
My unwearied course pursue!
Till, distinguished from afar,
My dear country rose to view;
Then quick descending from my airy height,
My pinions would I close, and stay my flight.

Euripides
c480-406BC

Thomas Gray
Portrait by John Giles Eccardt, 1747-1748

Luna Habitabilis (An Extract)
Thomas Gray

Thomas Gray was born in 1716, the fifth of twelve children born to Philip and Dorothy Gray and the only one to survive infancy. At the age of 11 he was sent to Eton from where he went up to Pembroke College, Cambridge in 1734. A deeply intellectual young man he wrote to his friends that there he found the Masters "mad with pride" and the Fellows "sleepy, drunken, dull, illiterate Things". Gray went on to become one of England's most prolific and famous poets.

It was in 1737 at Pembroke that he wrote the 95-line Latin poem *Luna Habitabilis (The Moon is Inhabited)* which was published in *Musae Etonenses*. Many hold the view that the last six lines, of which a very loose translation has become famous, was a prophecy of The Battle of Britain.

> Foedera mox icta, et Gemini commercial mundi,
> Agminaque assiueto glomerata sub aethere cerno.
> Anglia, quae pelagi jamdudum torquet habernas,
> Exercetque frequens ventos, atque imperat undae;
> Aeris attollet fasces, veteresque triumphos
> Huc etiam feret, et victis dominabitur auris.

The translation of these lines is

> The time will come, when thou shalt lift thine eyes
> To watch a long-drawn battle in the skies,
> While aged peasants, too amazed for words,
> Stare at the flying fleet of wondrous birds,
> England, so long mistress of the sea,
> Where winds and waves confess her sovereignty,
> Her ancient triumphs yet on high shall bear,
> And reign, the sovereign of the conquered air.

Thomas Gray
1716-1771

William Wordsworth, 1770-1850

Peter Bell – Prologue (an extract)
William Wordsworth

I found four verses of this poem in Stella Wolfe Murray's delightful anthology *The Poetry of Flight* published in 1925, but on reading the whole Prologue felt that this wonderful vision of earthly and inter-planetary flight deserved the thirteen that I have chosen.

Born in 1770, William Wordsworth was appointed Distributor of Stamps for Westmoreland in 1813, for which office he was paid £400 per annum which gave him financial security but made him the butt of his fellow poets. This 'treachery' was compounded when he campaigned for Tory politicians in the 1818 and 1820 elections.

In 1819 Wordsworth dedicated his long poem *Peter Bell* to Robert Southey, the Poet Laureate whom he succeeded on Southey's death in 1843.

There's something in a flying horse
  There's something in a huge balloon,
But through the clouds I'll never float
Until I have a little boat
  Whose shape is like a crescent-moon.

And now I 'have' a little Boat,
  In shape a very crescent-moon
Fast through the clouds my boat can sail;
But if perchance your faith should fail,
  Look up – and you shall see me soon!

The woods my friends are round you roaring,
  Rocking and roaring like a sea;
The noise of danger's in your ears,
And ye have all a thousand fears
  Both for my little boat and me.

Meanwhile untroubled I admire
  The pointed horns of my canoe;
And, did not pity touch my breast,
To see how ye are all distrest,
  Till my ribs ached, I'd laugh at you!

Away we go, my Boat and I –
  Frail man ne-er sate in such another;
Whether among the winds we strive,
Or deep into the clouds we dive,
  Each is contented with the other.

Away we go – and what care we
  For treasons, tumults, and for wars?
We are as calm in our delight
As is the crescent-moon so bright
  Among the scattered stars.

Up goes my boat among the stars,
  Through many a breathless field of light
Through many a long blue field of ether
Leavening the thousand stars beneath her,
  Up goes my little boat so bright.

The Crab, the Scorpion and the Bull –
  We pry among them all; have shot
High o'er the red-haired race of Mars,
Covered from top to toe with scars;
  Such company I like it not!

The towns in Saturn are decayed,
  And melancholy spectres throng them; --
The Pleiads, that appear to kiss
Each other in the vast abyss
  With joy I sail among them.

Swift Mercury resounds with mirth,
  Great Jove is full of stately bowers;
But these and all that they contain,
What are they to that tiny grain,
  That little earth of ours?

Then back to Earth, the dear green Earth: --
  Whole ages if I here should roam,
The world for my remarks and me
Would not a whit the better be;
  I've left my heart at home.

See! there she is, the matchless earth!
  There spreads the famed Pacific Ocean,
Old Andes thrusts yon craggy spear
Thro' the grey clouds – the Alps are here
  Like waters in commotion.

Yon tawny slip is Libya's sands –
  That silver thread the river Dnieper
And look, where clothed in brightest green
Is a sweet isle, of isles the queen;
  Ye fairies, from all evil keep her.

William Wordsworth
1770-1850

The Right Honourable The Lord Tennyson FRS
1869 carbon print by Julia Margaret Cameron

Locksley Hall (an extract)
Alfred, Lord Tennyson

Alfred Tennyson was born in 1809 when his father was rector of Somersby in Lincolnshire. He entered Trinity College, Cambridge in 1827, the same year that he and his brother published their first collection of poetry entitled *Poems by Two Brothers*. Alfred's poetry flourished and he became one of the most popular writers in the English language. Following Wordsworth's death in 1850, Tennyson was appointed Poet Laureate, a position he held for 42 years. He was buried in Westminster Abbey and succeeded in the title by his son Hallam who became second Governor-General of Australia.

Tennyson wrote Locksley Hall in 1842, 61 years before the Wright brothers made the first sustained flight of a heavier than air machine, universally recognised as being the beginning of powered flight, and almost 100 years before the Battle of Britain. His prophecies of the coming of aviation, aerial warfare and the United Nations are nothing short of incredible.

Men, my brothers, men the workers, ever reaping something new:
That which they have done but earnest of the things that they shall do:
For I dipped into the future, far as human eye could see,
Saw the vision of the world, and all the wonder that would be;
Saw the heavens fill with commerce, argosies of magic sails,
Pilots of the purple twilight, dropping down with costly bales;
Heard the heavens fill with shouting, and there rained a ghastly dew

From the nations' airy navies grappling in the central blue;
Far along the world wide whisper of the south-wind rush-
ing warm
With the standards of the peoples plunging through the
thunder-storm;
Till the war-drum throbbed no longer, and the battle flag
was furled
In the Parliament of man, the Federation of the world.

Alfred, Lord Tennyson
1809-1892

Prophecy
William H Rhodes

William Henry Rhodes was born in Windsor, North Carolina in 1822. Having 'great ambition and a mind superior to his companions, he became a leader among the young men of Galveston... and gathered around him an association of young men whose zealous natures were congenial to his lofty ambition'. He entered Harvard law school and then practised Law in North Carolina before sailing for California, then considered to be the new El Dorado.

In July, 1869, he witnessed the flight of Frederick Marriott's unmanned, steam powered dirigible, the first powered flight in America, and this was probably the inspiration for his prophecy which he wrote about 1874 and which was first published in the year of his death, 1876.

Why his seventh verse should consist of only four lines is a mystery...

Hurrah for the wings that never tire –
  For the nerves that never quail;
For the heart that beats in a bosom of fire –
  For the lungs whose cast-iron lobes respire
  Where the eagle's breath would fail!

As the genii bore Aladdin away,
  In search of his palace fair,
On his magical wings to the land of Cathay,
  So here I will spread out my pinions today
  On the cloud-born billows of air.

Up! Up! To its home on the mountain crag –
  Where the condor builds its nest,
I mount far fleeter than hunted stag,
  I float far higher than Switzer flag,
  Hurrah for the lightning's guest!

Away, over steeple and cross and tower –
  Away, over river and sea:
I spurn at my feet the tempests that lower,
  Like minions base of a vanquished power,
  And mutter their thunders at me!

Diablo frowns as above him I pass,
Still loftier heights to attain;
Calavera's groves are but blades of grass –
Yosemite's sentinel peaks a mass
Of ant-hills dotting a plain!

Sierra Nevada's shroud of snow,
  And Utah's desert sand,
Shall never turn backward the flow
  Of that human tide that may come and go
  To the vales of the sunset land!

Wherever the coy earth veils her face –
  Where polar pallors her blushes efface,
Or tropical blooms lend her beauty and grace –
  I can flutter my plumage there!

Where the Amazon rolls through a mystic land –
  Where Chiapas buried her dead –
Where central Australian deserts expand –
  Where Africa seethes in Saharas of sand –
  Even there shall my pinions spread!

No longer shall earth with her secrets beguile,
  For I, with undazzled eyes,
Will trace to their souces the Niger and Nile,
  And stand without dread on the boreal isle,
  The Colon of the skies!

Then hurrah for the wings that never tire –
  For the sinews that never quail;
For the heart that throbs in a bosom of fire –
  For the lungs whose cast-iron lobes respire
  Where the eagle's breath would fail!

William H Rhodes
1822-1876

Humbert Wolfe by Sir William Rothenstein, chalk, 1931

The First Airman
Humbert Wolfe

Humbert Wolfe was an unlikely author of such a moving piece of poetry. Never an aviator himself, he was an Italian-born civil servant from a Jewish family and worked in the Board of Trade and the Ministry of Labour where his career was recognised by the award of a CBE and a CB.

He was, however, a hugely popular man of letters in the 1920s, and a prolific author of poetry, translations and novels.

I have picked his poem as the harbinger of Man's conquest of the air and his first line for the title of this anthology.

Give me the wings, magician. I will know
What blooms on airy precipices grow
That no hand plucks, large unexpected blossoms,
Scentless with cry of curlews in their bosoms,
And the great winds like grasses where their stems
Spangle the universe with diadems.
I will pluck those flowers and those grasses, I
Icarus, drowning upwards through the sky
With air that closes underneath my feet
As water above a diver. I will meet
Life with the dawn in heaven, and my fingers
Dipped in the golden floss of hair that lingers
Across the unveiled spaces and makes them colder,
As a woman's hair across her naked shoulder,
Death with the powdered stars will walk and pass
Like a man's breath upon a looking-glass,
For a suspended heart-beat making dim
Heaven brighter afterwards because of him.

Give me the wings, magician. So their tune
Mix with the silver trumpets of the moon,
And, beyond music mounting, clean outrun
The golden diapason of the sun.
There is a secret that the birds are learning
Where the long lanes in heaven have a turning
And no man yet has followed; therefore these
Laugh hauntingly across our usual seas.
I'll not be mocked by curlews in the sky;
Give me the wings, magician, or I die.

His call for wings or death was heard, and thus
Came both to the first airman, Icarus.

Humbert Wolfe, CB, CBE
1885-1940

Icarus
Christian Hamilton

I chose this poem from the anthology of the same name which was only available in the library at RAF Cranwell; it has neither rhyme nor meter, but the emotion and the sentiment are compelling.

Researching the poet proved difficult and I was astonished to find that he was General Sir Ian Standish Monteith Hamilton, GCB, GCMG, DSO, Gordon Highlanders, and son of Colonel Christian Monteith Hamilton, who had commanded the 92nd Highlanders, later the Gordon Highlanders. Described contemporarily as "a gallant officer, Scottish gentleman and man of letters" Sir Ian's distinguished army career ended with the disastrous expedition to Gallipoli where he was in command from April, 1915 to the following October.

Icarus was first published in his collection of poetry in 1887. Why the general used his father's Christian name as a nom-de-plume is, to me, a mystery. The poem could well serve as his own epitaph.

Gods: I have flown!
All my young body is broken on the rocks
And all the red cliffs swim before my eyes –
The summer haze, perhaps – or my sight fails –
Dim world, these eyes of mine shall open soon
On great Olympus. Hah! I shall tell Jove
That I have flown – I, Icarus, a mortal!
Oh, the sun burns down pitiless upon me
And on my crushed white wings – my wings – my wings –
Why did I fly so high? I might by now
Be safe, if only – only – Ah, but FLYING
High and yet higher into the burning blue
Above the ochre crags and jade green sea!
How could I help it – how do otherwise?

Sir Ian Hamilton by Sir William Rothenstein, pencil, 1916

And when the softening wax upon my shoulders
Let the great plumes slip sideways and I fell
Hardly was terror there. I saw the rocks
Rush up to meet me, and I knew that never
Never would Icarus rise again.

But I have flown – have flown. These are my wings,
All crushed and torn and dabbled – they are wings,
And this day on Olympus Jove shall know...
How the cliffs shudder... and the sun is scorching...
Pain stabs my broken body so – I die –
Gods: I have flown!

General Sir Ian Hamilton, GCB, GCMG, DSO
1853-1947

Lines on Aerostation
Amelia

This charming poem is from *The Crowded Sky*, first published by Cassell in 1959 and edited by Neville Duke and Edward Lanchbery. They in turn found it in the delightfully named *The Straggling Astrologer of the Nineteenth Century*; or, *Magazine of Celestial Intelligences*, No. 15, September 11, 1824. Essentially a poem about ballooning it captures the poetry of flight whatever the means of getting airborne.

I am unable to discover the identity of Amelia.

While thus on high the silken castle glides,
Bright as a meteor, through the azure tides;
O'er towns, and towers, and temples, wins its way,
Or mounts sublime, and gilds the vault of day;
Silent, with upturned eyes, unbreathing crowds
Pursue the floating wonder to the clouds;
And, flushed with transport, or benumbed with fear,
Watch, as it rises, the diminished sphere.
Now less and less – and now, a speck is seen –
And now the fleeting rack obtrudes between!
The calm adventurer in ether sails,
Views broader stars, and breathes in purer gales;
Sees, like a map, in many a waving line,
Round earth's blue plains, her lucid waters shine;
Sees, at his feet, the forky lightnings glow,
And hears innocuous thunders roar below.
Rise, great Adventurer! Urge thy vent'rous flight
High o'er the Moon's pale ice-reflected light!
High o'er the pearly star, whose beamy horn
Hangs in the east, gay harbinger of morn!
Leave the fair beams, which issuing from afar,

Play with new lustres round the Georgian star;
Shun, with strong oars, the Sun's attractive throne,
The sparkling zodiac, and the milky zone,
Where headlong comets, with increasing force,
Through other systems bend their blazing course.
For thee, Cassiope her chair withdraws;
For thee the Bear retracts his shaggy paws;
High o'er the north thy golden orb shall roll,
And blaze eternal round the wond'ring Pole.
So Argo, rising from the southern main,
Lights, with new stars, the blue ethereal plain;
With favouring beams the mariner protects,
And the bold course which first it steered directs.

Amelia

The Pioneers
1903-1914

Introduction

Gliders were the true fore-runners of the aeroplane and the German pioneer, Otto Lilienthal, led the field between 1891 and 1896, being described by Wilbur Wright as 'easily the most important pioneer in this field'. His famous book *Birds as the Basis of Aviation*, published in 1889, summed up his approach to solving the problems of human flight.

With the advent of a simple motor car engine the realisation of man's dream to fly took place on the sands at Kitty Hawk on 17th December, 1903, when the Wright Brothers made the first controlled, powered and sustained heavier than air human flight.

The Wrights were quickly followed by pioneers in Europe where France led in aviation and Deperdussin, Morane-Saulnier and Bleriot became household names. Britain was not far behind and Thomas Sopwith, Geoffrey de Havilland, Oswald Short, Alliot Verdon Roe and others took up the challenge.

During the next decade the pioneers concentrated on turning their flimsy craft into sturdy airframes and their motors, from inefficient and unreliable power-plants only just able to lift them into the air, into engines capable of sustained operation at ever-increasing altitudes and over ever lengthening journeys in all weathers.

Flight, a weekly periodical devoted to the new science of aviation, made its first appearance on 7th January, 1909, and chronicled these pioneering efforts. It has remained for more than a century the leading British aviation publication.

The poetry of this era was romantic and glorified the bravery, even impetuosity, of the pioneers, concentrating on the novelty and the wonders of this new world or the deaths of these young men, an all too common feature of Man's incursion into the new medium of the air.

FLIGHT

DECEMBER 10, 1910.

THE SANDERS "TEACHER."

THOSE wishing to take up aviation either as a recreation or a profession find many drawbacks at the commencement of their undertaking, but one of the most formidable, especially to those not

The Sanders Teacher in use.

blessed with a long purse, is the risk of smashing the machine while endeavouring to learn how to control and fly it.

Even the most apt pupil is certain to find himself in difficulties at some time or another during his probation, and owing to lack of skill the machine is necessarily sacrificed to save his life, or at least to prevent a serious accident. The invention, therefore, of a device which will enable the novice to obtain a clear conception of the workings of the control of an aeroplane, and of the conditions existent in the air, without any risk personally or otherwise, is to be

THE SANDERS TEACHER.—The Pivoted Rocker.

welcomed without a doubt. Several have already been constructed to this end, and the Sanders Teacher is the latest to enter the field.

The aim and object of an invention of this kind is naturally to render tuition safe to the pupil while at the same time giving him confidence. Now there is a tendency to design such an apparatus merely for purposes of balance and without any real resemblance to an actual aeroplane, while the very balance is so exaggerated that the pupil is placed under conditions that are in no way so arduous in free flight.

The Sanders Teacher seeks to overcome both these difficulties. In the first place the teacher so closely adheres to the construction of the actual aeroplane that the pupil in learning to control it is simultaneously learning the control of the machine he wishes to pilot, and the principle is applicable to any make or type of aeroplane. In the second place the balance of the teacher is so arranged on scientific principles that the conditions are practically the same as if the pupil were actually in the air. The varying force of the wind has effect in almost an identical manner as on a working aeroplane, while the niceties of lateral and longitudinal stability are not carried to an extreme.

The device, as will be realised from the description following, is neither costly nor elaborate, while the perfection of workmanship to be found in the Sanders biplane is also plainly noticeable here. One would say that the motto of the firm is "If a thing is worth doing at all it is worth doing well," as even the minutest detail is carried out with most scrupulous care and accuracy and only incorporated in the construction after much thought and experiment.

The machine consists of a fuselage-elevator, two lateral ailerons and a rudder either single or double planed. The control is a simple motor steering wheel in front of the pupil connected up with elevator, rudder and ailerons. All these details are standard parts of the Sanders biplane and can be substituted if desired by the same parts of any other type of aeroplane. Thus, the purchaser of a Teacher is buying parts which can be used later if he wishes in the construction of a machine and his outlay can therefore scarcely be considered an extravagant one. The fuselage is slung on to a wooden pivot consisting of a hexagonal bottom on which a crossway square running on wheels is placed. Above this is a rocker bearing a flat board surmounted by two triangular brackets with a bar running through sockets at the top. This bar also passes through two corresponding sockets on the upper part of the fuselage which is thus slung on the pivot. A bolt runs vertically through the centre of the pivot, beneath the rocker, on which the entire machine can swing round to the wind, the movement being very free owing to the ball bearings on the crossway piece below. The ailerons attached at either end of two 12 ft. spars are braced up by means of wire stays to the fuselage and a mast is situated at the rear of the machine. They are also supported above by a rubber spring attached to two small masts.

For the rest, a personal inspection is recommended to aviation instructors as a device worthy of their attention.

DOROTHY M. HAWARD.

⊛ ⊛ ⊛ ⊛

Artillery for Fighting Airships.

Two new weapons for offensive use against airships and aeroplanes have just been completed at the Krupp Works, Essen, and are now undergoing their tests. One of the guns is mounted on a completely armoured motor car, while the other, of a lighter type, is so arranged on the platform of a trailer, that it can be either used in that position or direct on the ground, it being provided with a carriage of the field artillery type, and the lurry fitted with runners for lowering the guns to the ground.

(Flight)

The Song of Aviators
Dorothy M Haward

Flight magazine's first issue was on 2nd January, 1909. During a short span of barely a year a lady called Dorothy M Haward wrote for the magazine. An article in the 10th December, 1910 issue, describing the 'Sanders Teacher', a primitive flying simulator, showed that she had technical capability, but it was her poetry about this pioneering era of flying that caught my eye. I have failed to discover anything about her and why she only wrote for a year but her poetry has a timeless quality. Her first poem was published on 20th August, 1910.

This is the song of those who dare,
  The dauntless and the free,
Who fight the armies of the air,
  As we have fought the sea.

Honour to those who on the wing
  Thus earn the laurel crown,
The empires of the world shall sing
  The songs of their renown.

We are the pioneers
  Who seek the Air King's throne,
That you in after years
  May claim it for your own.

The dauntless courage ours,
  Whose purpose is unchanged,
Though death and all his powers
  Against ourselves are ranged.

We brave the Storm Fiend's might,
  The tempest and the rains.
Night hears our throbbing flight,
  Day sees our snowy planes.

You conquered heat and steam,
  The lightning's lurid fire.
The ocean and the stream,
  Are slaves to your desire.

But greater things we do,
  And greater perils dare,
Who strive to win for you
  The kingdoms of the air.

We glory in our task –
  To make the winds your slaves,
And no reward we ask,
  Save that of honoured graves.

Dorothy M. Haward

The Ballad of the Aeroplane
Dorothy M Haward

In their 14th September, 1910 issue *Flight* published Dorothy's second poem.

A sweep, a swirl, a rush of air,
  Two wings that flutter in the blue,
Earth like a picture, far and fair,
  And then – unbounded space and you.
  Perchance some bird may pause to view
Your coming in its rapid flight,
  Then leave you free to dare and do
In these great worlds of Space and Light.

Swift, high and sure you rise to where
  Your aeroplane flies straight and true,
Then, as you wish, descend, or bear
  Still onward for a mile or two.
Oh joy as you go swinging through
  The fresh, pure air, and what delight
To know you're free to dare and do
  In these great worlds of Space and Light.

Then let them say that we shall ne'er
  Be victors in this kingdom new,
Since earth and sea man's rule declare,
  The aerial world shall own it too.
The dreams and visions fancy drew,
  Shall be revealed to human sight,
And we be free to dare and do
  In these great worlds of Space and Light.

Envoi

Though now the pioneers are few,
  Soon will the dawn rise fair and bright,
When all are free to dare and do
  In these great worlds of Space and Light.

Dorothy M Haward

Ferat Palmam Qui Meruit
Dorothy M Haward

A month later Dorothy was moved to write a requiem poem for pioneer aviators using as her title the ancient Spartan motto "Let he who merits the palm possess it".

O, weep for the brave, for our noble and best,
Who have flown their last flight and found their last rest.
The engines are stilled that were throbbing of yore,
The wide planes are shattered to flutter no more.

O, weep for the brave, for the seekers of truth,
Who yielded their lives in the flower of their youth,
And lay on the grave of each well honoured name
A circlet of laurel – the guerdon of fame.

O, weep for the brave who have striven that we
As lords of the air in the future may be.
O, shame on the world that has nothing but sneers
For what they accomplished, the brave pioneers.

O, weep for the brave, but of joy be your tears,
They reap the rich harvest of nobly spent years.
O, happy are they who have died in the hour
When triumph was theirs and the fulness of power.

Dorothy M Haward

Hard Work Ahead: Mr. A. V. Roe standing in front of one of his early machines after a fairly typical landing. It is thought that the A.I.D. would not have passed the construction.

["FLIGHT" *Photograph*

GORDON-BENNETT RACE AT EASTCHURCH.—Mr. Gustav Hamel and his 100-h.p. Blériot just before his start in the race. On the right he is just away, to be brought down, however, after three-quarters of a minute, after rounding the first mark tower, as seen in the wreckage below. Note the rolling method of the assistants in clearing the machine at the moment of starting.

AV Roe and Gustav Hamel with their
'Inconstant Lady Aeroplanes'
(Flight)

Ballad (From any Aviator to any Aeroplane)

Dorothy M Haward

A month later Dorothy penned this enchanting little poem. Like ships and boats before them, aeroplanes had quickly acquired the female gender. In view of the need in modern times to respect political correctness I will not comment further but leave Dorothy to relate how the aviators of the day viewed this matter.

No maiden ears have heard my vows
  Of changeless love and fealty,
And yet mine is the fairest spouse
  Man ever had on land or sea.
I wooed her in the summer sun,
  I wooed her in the winter rain,
And now I know at last I've won
  My matchless Lady Aeroplane.

Her planes are snowy white in hue,
  And her propeller's perfect quite,
Angle and balance both are true,
  Her engine is a pure delight.
Forgotten now are all the years
  I wooed and strove for her in vain,
And vanished too my doubts and fears –
  She's mine – my Lady Aeroplane.

Though other men perchance may claim,
  That they have found a bride as fair,
'Tis you who brought me joy and fame,
  And none can rival you I swear.
So flying gaily on we two
  Laugh at the others with disdain,
There's nothing that we cannot do,
  I and my Lady Aeroplane.

Envoi
(After the smash.)

Women are fickle so they say,
  And wooing them is scarce a gain,
But you are fickler far than they,
  Inconstant Lady Aeroplane.

Dorothy M Haward

Issy-Les-Moulineaux

21st May, 1911

Dorothy M Haward

At 6 o'clock in the morning of Sunday, 21st May, 1911, a crowd of 200,000 people gathered on the airfield at Issy-les-Moulineaux to watch the start of the Paris – Madrid air race. Four of the nine entrants took off. The fifth, a monoplane designed, built and flown by Emile Louis Train, started it's take-off run just as, astonishingly, a platoon of mounted cuirassiers who had been ordered to clear the runway, trotted onto it, followed by several VIPs who wanted to stretch their legs. Failing to take off the aeroplane crashed into the VIPs. The French Minister of War, Maurice Berteaux was killed and President Monis was badly injured. The race was abandoned. Dorothy wrote this touching epitaph for the 27th May issue of *Flight*.

France, your history has shown us all through the distant ages,
  How your sons can conquer in courage and high emprise;
And not the least of their deeds written upon these pages
  Stands the hour when we hailed you – Queen of the virgin skies.

France, when the world thought flight only man's idle dreaming,
  You without pause or falter challenged the Great Unknown,
Dauntless in spite of failure, testing, proving, and scheming,
  So that the present reaps the harvest the past has sown.

France, you have nobly heard the call of a High Endeavour,
  Paying to Death the toll of many an honoured name,
And all the wondering world holds you now and for ever
  Worthy of your triumph, worthy of all your fame.

MAY 27, 1911.

FLIGHT

THE TRAIN MONOPLANE.—View from in front of the Train monoplane which was involved in the catastrophe at Issy at the start of the Paris–Madrid Race. M. Train has embodied in his design a system of under-carriage somewhat similar to that evolved by M. Pischoff, the aviator being seated below the plane and protected by the covered-in body.

Train Crash

French Cuirassiers surround Louis Train's monoplane after the crash

France, we paid you our homage, there on the cliffs of Dover,
  When the distance was spanned that separates shore from
    shore;
Every triumph you showed us, hailed we the wide world over,
  Prouder to be your friend than ever we were before.

France, in your hour of mourning, England extends her pity,
  Sorrows for your disaster, bowing for you her head;
From the heart of her people, village and town and city,
  Take the wreath of their tears as worthy to crown your dead.

Dorothy M Haward

The Conquest of the Air

(A Song of the Winds)

Dorothy M Haward

Dorothy's last poem in the year that she wrote for *Flight* appeared in the 8th July, 1911 issue of the magazine. No reason is given for her writing it and there is no record of the reason for her ceasing to write for the magazine. Had the short year been too full of tragedy? Had she been close to Cecil Grace (see *Requiescat*, p.313)? Sadly we shall never know. If she did stop writing aviation poetry this is a fitting epitaph.

Wind from the Realms of Silence,
  Lord of the Frozen North,
Back in the far dim ages
  You sent your challenge forth.
Your ice-strewn seas are vanquished,
  Your endless wastes of snow,
And soon your aerial kingdom
  Victorious man shall know.

Wind from the scorching desert
  And trackless forest zone,
Foul swamps where death lies lurking
  To claim man for his own.
Unheeding of the perils,
  Man forced a highway through,
And soon his planes shall hover
  In your unconquered blue.

Wind from the broad Atlantic
  Whose mighty billows roar,
And thunder their defiance
  Along our western shore.
What though your waves may scatter
  Our vessels on the Main,
Man seeks a new dominion,
  His ship the Aeroplane.

Wind from the North Sea reaches,
  Wind of the frost and gales,
Whose rude breath swept the Goodwins
  And filled the Vikings' sails.
Your lofty throne is shaken,
  Full soon shall you declare
Man's last and greatest triumph,
  The conquest of the air.

Dorothy M Haward

Flying
Mark Kerr, 1912

Mark Kerr was born in 1864, the son of Admiral Lord Frederick Kerr. Mark joined the Royal Navy at the age of 13, serving during the Egyptian War of 1882 and in the Sudan in 1891. After several appointments as naval attaché he was promoted to Admiral and in 1913 he became Commander-in-Chief of the Royal Hellenic Navy, a post he retained until 1915. He was awarded his Aviator's certificate in 1914, at the age of 50, and was the first British flag officer to become a pilot. Commander-in-chief of the British Adriatic Squadron in 1917 and 1918, he was seconded to the Air Board to help form the Air Ministry and the Royal Air Force, for which purpose he was granted the rank of Major-General. He retired from the RAF towards the end of 1918, becoming a writer. He died in 1944 at the age of 79.

His poem captures the excitement and novelty of an early flight in an aircraft of the Royal Naval Air Service; written two years before he himself became a pilot.

Over the hills and far away, resting by night and flying by day,
For strength of nerve and power of wing
Blending together make the Air – King.

Winding! Whirring! Rolling! Bumping!
Running! Rushing! Lifting! Jumping!
Springing to life, the plane is clear
Gliding swiftly into air
Like a swallow skimming fleet,
O'er the cornstooks bound in thrave:
Sinks the ground beneath your feet
Like a fast receding wave.

Banking! Turning! Slipping! Climbing!
Warping! Wheeling! Dipping! Diving!
And the pulse of the flier
Is faster, faster beating
As higher, higher, higher
The monoplane is fleeting
Through the quickly rarefying air.

Oh! The humming in the wires
Of the wind that never tires
And the crooning of the wings
And the sobbing and the sighing
Of the gusts through which you're flying
And the tune the tractor sings.
As the air goes past a-rushing
While the clouds your wings are brushing
With the rain that sharply stings.

Rush! Rush! Rush! Higher! Higher! Higher!
The bumping and the jumping and the swaying,
While the rain is a-spraying and the hail is a-flaying.
Higher! Higher! Higher! Wings that never tire
To climb o'er the clouds to the sun,
And the tips of the planes appear and disappear
As you madly drive along through the mist enladen'd air
With the cracking of the Gnome and the whirring of the screw
And the humming and the drumming of the air you're tearing through.

Out of the storm-cloud into the sun
Smoother and smoother the Air-bird doth run
Quietly stealing across the blue sky
Out-pacing the eagle the Air-craft will fly;
Caring for nothing in Heaven or Earth
For this is a new life come into birth.

Admiral Mark Kerr, CB, CVO, RN, 1864-1944
From the portrait by Gabriella Fabricotti, 1916

Sailing across the country
On new found wings of the wind,
Gulping the miles behind her
Hurling the league behind,
Vain is the mail train's effort,
Futile the motor's speed,
Distance is only a banquet
Supplying the Air-bird's need.

Sailing over the ocean
Where the great ships plough their way
Whence sails have almost vanished
While the steamers have their day.
But the smoke ascends with a question
Up through the pellucid air,
"Who tries to rival our powers?
Our supremacy, Who will dare!"

But the monster quakes in her engines
For she knows that her utmost pace
Of twenty-five knots to the hour
Will avail her nought in the race
With the strange Air-craft above her
Who trebles her speed with ease
And flies the water at ninety knots
Helped by a favouring breeze.

The sea has fled behind her,
The shore is drawing near
And the chosen place of landing
To the pilot's eye is clear.
Suddenly stopped is the engine,
Ceases the buzzing and riot –
Falls on the soul of the pilot
A feeling of infinite quiet.
The earth rushes up to meet him
As he planes with the engine still

And he turns to the right and the left hand
Curbing her might to his will.
Then just as she seems to be touching
He brings her tail to the ground
And skims once again like a Swallow
Till the chassis the landing has found,
Then rolling across the surface
She gently brings up to rest
As the wandering Peregrine Falcon
Returns at eve to her nest.

Admiral Mark Kerr, CB, CVO
1864-1944

The Charted Skies
C L O'Donnell

O'Donnell's poem is a reminder that migrating birds have, for millennia, flown the skies into which the aspiring aviator is about to launch himself. (See *Flying Machines*, p.257)

Before you took the heavens at a bound –
Young airman, with the star-winds in your hair –
You had precursors on the floods of air;
Those deeps no plummet made of man can sound
Yielded a roadstead all the birds had found
Out of creation's morning. Free and fair
Their sails were spread or any mariner
With Viking triumph of the sky was crowned.
Spring after Spring they tack into the gale,
The fleets of robins, bluebirds flying north, -
Who marked the course that these armadas sail,
Who bids their comings and their goings forth?
There where your wings break on resisting tides
The frail craft of the swallow dreaming rides.

C L O'Donnell

Youth and Flight
Clarence Winchester

Clarence (Arthur Charles) Winchester was born in Notting Hill Gate, London, in 1895. He learned to fly in 1913. A prolific author and journalist he wrote on aeronautics for the *Daily Mail* and was a founder member of the original Institute of Aeronautical Engineers and an associate of the Royal Aeronautical Society. He rose to be Chief Editor of the Amalgamated Press and produced many books on Flying including *Wonders of World Aviation* in 1938. After the Second World War he became Literary Editor of the *Daily Sketch* and wrote extensively for American newspapers and magazines. He used the pen-name 'Ornis' and the pseudonym C. Tanner-Rutherford. This poem is from his *Poems of an Air Pilot*, published in 1921.

Brave youth aglow with ecstasy has borne
  Himself upon frail wings of gossamer –
  No fear within his breast less he should err,
And failing, from this ecstasy be torn.
Through the red dawn when birds were carolling
  Oft has he soared, as they, to some proud height
  Above ignoble things, and in his flight
Revealed the strength of man all-conquering.

Now have the long dreams of a thousand years
  Come true, and down the lovely windswept skies
  He leaps anew with laughter in his eyes,
And on his cheeks the warmth of happy tears;
For youth, no more restrained than his own thought,
Has shattered bound'ries and his freedom wrought.

Clarence Winchester
1895-1981

Conquerors
Angela Morgan

Angela Morgan was an American, born in 1875, who, throughout her life earned a precarious living as a writer and poet. Her entry in *Philosopedia* describes her as "an eclectic in religious matters... she was strongly influenced by the American transcendentalist movement..... she came to regard poetry as a vehicle for the expression of cosmic truths and ultimately for the spiritual transformation of mankind. The messianic element in her thought was strengthened in her later years by a series of mystical experiences... she finally became convinced that she was in direct contact with the cosmic forces which created the universe. She was a social visionary who opposed war, capital punishment, the economic exploitation of the poor, and the oppression of women, and who pleaded, in her most serious poems, for a world of peace, social justice and human brotherhood. Although widely published in popular magazines and the author of many volumes of poems and other writings, she was not regarded by her peers as a poet of the front rank. She remained aloof from the main current of the modern poetry movement... never venturing herself into free verse or exploring new forms of poetic expression. She remained firmly within the classical tradition of the heroic couplet and the sonnet in the manner of Pope and Coleridge."

She was awarded an honorary degree (Litt.D.) by the Golden State University, Los Angeles and was elected poet laureate of the National Federation of Women's Clubs.

Ye who ascend into the cosmic blue,
Pledged to the glory of a mighty cause,
Clean-stript of cowardice, of self devoid,
Laughing to see the sudden yearning jaws
Of death below you in the swimming void,
How shall we name a tribute fit for you?
How shall we build a monument whose height
Shall match the marvel of your splendid flight?

Soldiers ye are, before whose glorious deed
Praise topples prone and petty lips are dumb.
Ye gladly forfeit life and all it brings,
That in the kindling centuries to come,
Men, free as gods, shall cleave the air with wings,
Shall stride their superstitions as a steed;
Mounting with ecstasy the waiting herds
Of willing clouds, unfettered as the birds.

Brave navigators ye, in ships of air,
Heralds of progress, servants of the race,
Great as Columbus was and yet more bold,
Ye plumb the regions of uncharted space
That millions now unborn shall yet be told
How mind has conquered matter everywhere!
Ye dare, that man shall see himself supreme,-
Lord of the Air, and Master of his Dream.

Angela Morgan
1875-1957

In the Air
Lord Gorell

In July, 1921, Lord Gorell was appointed Under-Secretary of State for Air in the coalition government of Lloyd George. As well as being a politician with a seat on the Liberal benches in the House of Lords he was an author of many works of fiction and several collections of poetry.

I found the poem in Neville Duke's *The Crowded Sky*, but it originally appeared in Lord Gorell's *1904-1936 Poems*, published by John Murray in 1937, and was written as a celebration of his learning to fly in November, 1913.

Whir-r-r! Let her go! Hold off! Away!
She scuds out like a lizard from a stone!
Then – just as, by soft breezes blown
On autumn day,
The wads of thistle run and float –
She lifts: I am alone!
The fronting earth bends back from me,
So evenly, so suddenly
It is as if a giant smote
Hard on its verge –
And in a hurtling green the fields and foliage merge.

The wind is crashed asunder, surges, screams;
Behind me is a rushing, boiling roar;
I dip, and wheel, and sweep, and soar;
All heaven seems
To fall about me like a star,
In vastness evermore.
And I am strangely still; for I
Am hung within the moving sky

While all else yields to change: afar,
Deep miles below,
A little, huddling world is gliding slow.

Glory and freedom through my soul are driven:
I roam the kingdoms of uncharted space;
And, last in numbness turn my face
Down out of heaven;
The dark earth rushes up at me,
Then in a mighty race
Dives on beneath the flattening swoop;
The fields pour by, a frenzied troop –
The ground's light tremble suddenly!
The lizard's dart –
And all the realms of space lie dwindled and apart.

Ronald Barnes, 3rd Baron Gorell
1884-1963

Hamel's Departure
Nigel Norman

Nigel Norman was born in 1897; at 13 he went to Winchester and at 18 he joined the Royal Artillery, serving between 1915 and 1918. He then went up to Trinity College, Cambridge where he read engineering and architecture, graduating in 1922. In 1926 he learned to fly at Stag Lane and in a series of de Havilland Gipsy Moths he flew himself far and wide, visiting Salisbury, Southern Rhodesia and Hyderabad to design and build the airports there and Cairo, to found Misrair. In 1928, with others, he started Airwork.

His flying exploits deserve a book to themselves.

Nigel joined 601 (County of London) Squadron, Royal Auxiliary Air Force which he commanded in 1931. His three sons, Mark, Desmond and Torquil all served together in 601.

Gustav Hamel was born in 1899 of Danish parentage and, like Nigel Norman, was educated at Winchester School. Being eight years older than Norman, they would not have been contemporaries but Norman would certainly have heard of Hamel who learned to fly in 1910, the year that the Hamel family were granted British citizenship. His subsequent pioneering flights included delivery of the first official airmail, from Hendon to Windsor, a distance of 21 miles, and perfecting the art of looping. On 2nd January, 1914, he looped Miss Trehawke Davis, the first woman in the world to do so, and on 2nd February he performed fourteen loops over Windsor castle for King George V. His exploits would have inspired the 17 year old Norman.

In May, 1914, Hamel went to France to collect a new 80hp Morane-Saulnier monoplane. Despite the bad weather conditions he decided to take off for England.

June 21, 1913. FLIGHT

MEN OF MOMENT IN THE WORLD OF FLIGHT.

British Pilots.

MR. GUSTAV HAMEL.

665

As Hamel stood by the hangar door,
 Watching the troubled sky,
Francois, the head mechanic said:
 "M'sieu, the wind is high."
And the empty echo drifted back,
 "Too high!"

As the rising wind moaned round the eaves
 And the clouds went hurrying by,
The little dark mechanic man
 Asked him: "M'sieu will fly?"
And the hopeless echo wandered back
 "Will try."

But a smile spread over the young man's face
 And lit his steel grey eye,
And, laughing, he answered Francois back:
 "Yes, Francois, I will fly."
And the awful echo answered back
 "Will die!"

Air Commodore Sir Nigel Norman, RAF
1897-1943

"Flight" Copyright.

A characteristic attitude of Mr. Gustav Hamel after one of his remarkable flights at Hendon.

Hamel's Death (May 23rd 1914)
Nigel Norman

Despite the awful weather conditions Hamel decided to make the channel crossing in his new Morane-Saulnier monoplane. He took off on 23rd May from Paris and disappeared over the English Channel.

On 1st July of that year the crew of a French fishing boat found a body in the channel off Boulogne. They did not retrieve the body but from the clothing, a road map of Southern England, and "an inflated india rubber bicycle tube round the body which Mr. Morane, the eminent aeroplane designer induced him to wear when he left Paris", there was enough evidence for the Court to decide that it was Hamel.

As the swan's plumage white
Shines in the evening light
While his long, lonely flight
  Carries him northward,
So, Earth and Sky between
Hamel's fragile machine
That evening might be seen
  Hurrying forward.

As summer swallows go
Zigzagging to and fro,
Now high, now dipping low
  Over the water,
The frail craft goes rushing by,
Across the stormy sky
  Where the winds fought her.

At last the wind's dread wrath
Crumples the silk and lath
And on their downward path
  Faster and faster,
Pilot and wreck and all
In one last dizzy fall,
Through the mist's chilly pall
  Plunge to disaster.

Air Commodore Sir Nigel Norman, RAF
1897-1943

The First World War
1914-1918

Introduction

In the eleven years since the Wright Brothers' first flight, the aeroplane, like the submarine, had developed sufficiently to provide the military with new weapons with which to wage war. As the machine gun finally disposed of the cavalry and all the thrill and glamour that had accompanied that means of fighting, so the aeroplane became a replacement mount for a generation of young soldiers pressed into the first global conflict. Recruits to the Royal Flying Corps often came from cavalry regiments for the simple reason that the same qualities that made for a good horseman were also needed for a pilot – a good pair of hands, balance, a good seat and the courage that took a horseman across the hunting field or the field of battle. Early weaponry was crude – pilots and observers shot at each other with pistols and dropped small anti-personnel bombs by hand* – but it was thrilling nevertheless and a whole new environment in which a young man could win his spurs. Training was horrendously brief and casualties were resultantly high but this did nothing to curb the exultation for this new form of warfare, so the poetry of the time reflects the thrill as well as the fear of flying and man-to-man aerial combat.

With relatively few aircraft in the air at any one time pilots could still enjoy the freedom of flight and the scenery high above the carnage and horror of the trenches below and this is reflected in the poetry of Jeffery Day and Paul Bewsher. It is only later in the war, following the condemnation of civilian bombing from airships and the night bombing of cities, that the awful damage that could be inflicted on an unsuspecting population came to be realised, and out of that realisation grew the need for every nation to build an air force with which to defend its civilian population from aerial attack.

During the four years of the Great War of 1914 to 1918 each of the combatant nations poured money and effort into manufacturing and pressing into aerial service faster and more manoeuvrable fighter machines capable of out-flying the enemy, as well as bombers capable of carrying ever greater loads, in an effort to influence the course of the war. Advances in the new air arm of the services were spectacular, and the air ace was born, with Mannock, Ball, McCudden, Fonck, Guynemer and Nungesser vying for supremacy with Richthofen, Udet, Boelcke and Immelmann.

If John Gillespie Magee was the 'pilot poet' of the Second World War then among the far fewer pilots of the First World War that accolade must surely be shared by Jeffery Day and Paul Bewsher. Both were pilots in the Royal Naval Air Service, which was the forerunner of the Royal Flying Corps and the Royal Air Force. Like Magee, Day lived a tragically short life but, unlike Magee, Day lived long enough to prove himself in action. Bewsher, on the other hand, survived the war despite being shot down, and transferred to the Royal Air Force in 1918, leaving the service in 1919. This accounts for the fact that Bewsher's later poetry reflects a growing tiredness and realisation that the longer he flies in action the greater the chance of his being killed. Day's poetry, all written before he was 22, altogether lacks this quality.

* On 1st November, 1911, Lt. Giulio Gavotti dropped four light bombs from his Taube monoplane onto Turkish positions in Libya during the Italo-Turkish war and the age of aerial warfare began.

The Call of the Air
Jeffery Day, 1916-1917

Miles Jeffery Game Day was born at St. Ives, Huntingdon, on 1st December, 1896. Leaving Repton at the age of 18, he was commissioned into the Royal Naval Air Service as a Sub-Lieutenant. He was immediately recognised as an exceptional pilot and was chosen for test flying at sea that required high technical accomplishment, such as being launched in a Bristol Bullet from the top wing of a 'Baby' flying boat 50 miles off-shore. But Jeffery was impatient with the comparative inactivity of life at sea so he transferred to No.13 Squadron, RNAS, on the Western Front, always seeking action with the enemy and quickly being promoted to Flight Commander.

For his actions on 25th January and 2nd February, 1918 Jeffery was awarded the Distinguished Service Cross "for great skill and bravery as a fighting pilot". He was never to see the citation or receive the award. On 27th February, 1918, in his Commanding officer's words "he was shot down (in a Sopwith Camel) by six German aircraft which he attacked single-handed out to sea. He had out-distanced his flight, I think because he wished to break the (enemy's) formation, in order to make it easier for the less experienced people behind him to attack. He hit the enemy and they hit his machine which burst into flames; but, not a bit flurried, he nose-dived, flattened out, and landed perfectly on the water. He climbed out of his machine and waved his fellow-pilots back to their base; being in aeroplanes (not sea-planes) they could not assist him."

Day was shot down into the sea 25 miles off Dunkerque. Despite being dropped a life-jacket by fellow squadron pilots and an immediate and prolonged search being carried out, Jeffery was never found. He was 21.

His posthumous citation in the London Gazette of 16th March, 1918, read: "On January 25th he attacked single-handed six enemy

Flight Commander Jeffery Day, DSC, RNAS, 1896-1918

tri-planes, one of which he shot down; on February 2nd he attacked and destroyed an enemy two-seater machine on reconnaissance at 18,000 feet. He destroyed several enemy machines in a short space of time, and in addition had numerous indecisive engagements". He had a total of five victories.

Jeffery Day's poetry was eventually published in 1919 in a small book titled simply *Poems and Rhymes*. Erskine Childers, (*Riddle of the Sands*), himself an RNAS pilot wrote of Day "I think I was right in pronouncing him 'pure gold'. His air verses are the best I have seen".

In *Poems and Rhymes* a beautiful obituary written by a friend, only identified by the initials EHY, ends: "His service, done in the spirit in which he did it, requires more valour and endurance than have ever been required of man before. He met the new call and did more than meet it: he thrust ahead and with his poet's fire lit a new beacon on the path of duty. The memory of him and his fellow-knights will be the treasure of all English hearts in after time. We bear it in trust for them".

It is difficult to know which of Day's poems to celebrate first. I have chosen "The Call of the Air" which was the Duchess of Bedford's favourite, two verses of which she read in a BBC broadcast after her record breaking flight to India in 1929. She was later chided by a national newspaper for using the word 'damn' on the air!

Have you ever sat in crystal space, enjoying the sensations
Of an eagle hovered high above the earth,
Gazing down on man's ridiculous and infantile creations
And judging them according to their worth?
Have you looked upon a basin small enough to wash your face in,
With a few toys – ships collected by the shore,
And then realised with wonder that if those toys go under
Nine tenths of Britain's navy is no more.

Have you seen a khaki maggot crawling down a thread of cotton—
The route march of a regiment or so?
Have you seen the narrow riband, unimportant, half-forgotten,
That tells you that the Thames is far below?
Have you glanced with smiling pity at the world's most famous city,
A large grey smudge that barely strikes the eye?
Would you like to see things truly and appreciate them duly?
Well then do it, damn you, do it; learn to fly!

Have you left the ground in murkiness, all clammy, grey, and soaking,
And struggled through the dripping, dirty white?
Have you seen the blank sides closing in and felt that you were choking,
And then leapt into a land of blazing light
Where the burnished sun is shining on the clouds' bright silver lining,
A land where none but fairy feet have trod,
Where the splendour nearly blinds you and the wonder of it binds you,
And you know you are in heaven, close to God?

Have you tumbled from the sky until your wires were shrilly screaming,
And watched the earth go spinning round about?
Have you felt the hard air beat your face until your eyes were streaming?
Have you turned the solar system inside out?
Have you seen earth rush to meet you and the fields spread out to greet you,
And flung them back to have another try?
Would it fill you with elation to be boss of all creation?
Well then do it, damn you, do it; learn to fly!

Have you fought a dummy battle, diving, twisting, pirouetting,
At a lightning speed that takes away your breath?
Have you been so wildly thrilled that you have found yourself forgetting
That it's practice, not a battle to the death?
Have you hurtled low through narrow, tree-girt spaces like an arrow—
Seen things grow and disappear like pricked balloons?
Would you feel the breathless joys of it and hear the thrilling noise of it,
The swish, the roar, the ever-changing tunes?

Have you chased a golden sunbeam down a gold and silver alley,
With pink and orange jewels on the floor?
Have you raced a baby rainbow round a blue and silver valley,
Where purple caves throw back the engine's roar?
Have you seen the lights that smoulder on a cloud's resplendent shoulder
Standing out before a saffron-coloured sky?
Would you be in splendid places and illimitable spaces?
Well then do it, damn you, do it; learn to fly.

Flight Commander Jeffery Day, DSC, RNAS
1896-1918

On the Wings of the Morning
Jeffery Day, 1916-1917

In his obituary of Day, his friend E.H.Y. says "When he speaks of some wonderful flight through clouds and sunshine I can feel the air rushing past me and revel with him in the miracles of light and colour that he has seen."

A sudden roar, a mighty rushing sound
a jolt or two, a smoothly sliding rise.
a jumbled blur of disappearing ground,
and then all sense of motion slowly dies.
Quiet and calm the air slips past below,
as underneath a bridge still waters flow.

My turning wing inclines towards the ground;
The ground itself glides up with graceful swing
and at the plane's far tip twirls slowly round,
then drops from sight again beneath the wing
to slip away serenely as before,
a cubist-patterned carpet on the floor.

Hills gently sink and valleys fill.
The flattened fields grow infinitely small;
slowly they pass beneath and slower still
until they hardly seem to move at all.
Then suddenly they disappear from sight,
hidden by fleeting wisps of fading white.

The wing-tips, faint and dripping, dimly show,
blurred by the wreaths of mist that intervene.
Weird, half-seen shadows flicker to and fro
across the pallid fog-bank's blinding screen.
At last the choking mists release their hold,
And all the world is silver, blue, and gold.

The air is clear, more clear than sparkling wine;
  compared with this, wine is a turgid brew.
The far horizon makes a clean-cut line
  between the silver and the depthless blue.
    Out of the snow-white level reared on high
    glittering hills surge up to meet the sky.

Outside the wind screen's shelter gales may race:
  but in the seat a cool and gentle breeze
blows steadily upon my grateful face
  as I sit motionless and at my ease,
    contented just to loiter in the sun
    and gaze around me till the day is done.

And so I sit, half sleeping, half awake,
  dreaming a happy dream of golden days,
until at last, with a reluctant shake,
  I rouse myself, and with a lingering gaze
    at all the splendour of the shining plain
    make ready to come down to earth again.

The engine stops: a pleasant silence reigns –
  silence, not broken , but intensified
by the soft, sleepy wires' insistent strains,
  that rise and fall, as with a sweeping glide
    I slither down the well-oiled sides of space
    towards a lower less enchanted place.

The clouds draw nearer, changing as they come.
  Now, like a flash, fog grips me by the throat.
Down goes the nose: at once the wires' low hum
  begins to rise in volume and in note,
    till as I hurtle from the choking cloud
    it swells into a scream, high-pitched and loud.

The scattered hues and shades of green and brown
  fashion themselves into the land I know,
turning and twisting, as I spiral down
  towards the landing ground; till, skimming low,
    I glide with slackening speed across the ground,
    and come to rest with lightly grating sound.

Flight Commander Jeffery Day, DSC, RN
1896-1918

Bad Weather
Jeffery Day, 1916-1917

Every pilot knows the frustration of being grounded, waiting, sometimes almost interminably, for bad weather to clear!

To mope around
on the dull hard ground
very many weeks together
in the vilest weather
is a sad delay
for a pilot gay,
who is very nearly dying
for some complicated flying,
for the whizz! bang! crash!
and the hurricane's lash
and the wires that hum zoom! zoom!

When the weather is bad,
it's extremely sad
to recline at leisure
and to contemplate the pleasure
of the coughing scream
of a great sunbeam,
or the rumbling voice
of a good Rolls Royce,
or the buzzing drone
of a nice Le Rhone –
the extreme exhilaration
of a little aviation,
and the grip and tear
of the ice-cold air
and the wires that hum zoom! zoom!

Flight Commander Jeffery Day, DSC, RNAS
1896-1918

Coming Down
Jeffery Day, 1916-1917

I have a hand-painted wooden plaque on the door of my flight room which carries the motto "Flying is the second greatest thrill known to Man. Landing is the first". Jeffery Day expresses the sentiment more eloquently.

Whether it be by dives and swoops or a spin or a graceful
glide,
whether it be by a series of loops or one long breathless
slide,
as long as you know where you're trying to go
and go more or less where you're trying
if you want to come down, and you are coming down,
coming down is the best part of flying.

But whether it be a broken tail or a spar that carries away,
or whether it be your nerves that fail or a hidden flaw in a
stay,
when you're thoroughly in a wing-tip spin
and, no matter how hard you're trying,
you're still coming down and coming down,
then it's far the most damned part of flying.

And when you have been from dawn's first streak
in search of a submarine,
and you're hungry and bored and sick and weak
and there's never a thing to be seen,
till at last below the hangars show,
your wearied eyes consoling,
and you start to come down, then coming down
Is far the best part of patrolling.

But when there is nothing at all in sight and
you're many a mile from home,
and the rising sea is showing white and the breakers hiss
    and foam,
and your engines stop and you've got to drop
where the great grey waves are rolling,
and you've got to come down, then coming down
is the perfectest hell of patrolling.

And when you've done a three-hours' flight in the shell-
    infested skies,
numbed with cold of the awful height and the fear that
    petrifies,
when you know at last that the lines are past
and the phantom of death is fading,
how you love coming down, and fall three miles down! –
it is much the best part of raiding.

But if you are over hostile lands and you hear the
    shrapnel's dunt,
and you feel your controls go slack in your hands, or your
    engine stops with a grunt,
and you fear you are done and the Boche has won, and
    your hopes of return are fading,
how you hate coming down! but you've got to come down,
and that is the devil of raiding.

Flight-Commander Jeffery Day, DSC, RNAS
1896-1918

The Joys of Flying
Jeffery Day, 1916-1917

This final poem by Jeffery Day encapsulates all the passion that this young East Anglian, who loved country life, felt for flying. It builds up a wonderful galloping tempo that carries the reader along on a wave of enthusiasm and is a fitting epitaph for a brave naval aviator.

There is no pleasure a man may have on earth which can compare
in any way with a similar pleasure that he may have in the air,
wheresoever and whatsoever his dreams of bliss may be,
he would enjoy them more by air than he would by land or sea.
the thrill of a race or a breathless chase or the motion of galloping horses,
the sight of the ground as it streaks below and the dangers of hard ridden courses,
the feel of the clean cold air in his lungs and the slap of the air in his face,
the rhythm, the swing, the rip and the spring, and the dash of the wonderful pace,
such are joys that are hard to beat, such are pleasures indeed,
but in the air they are thrice as good, for they happen at thrice the speed.
The tense excitement, the savage hunts that big game shots adore,
the heavy silence shattered at last by the sudden grating roar,
the rustle of leaves and the stabbing light that splinters the solid black,
the lightning charge when death looms large, and the rifle's vengeful crack,
the howl of the wolf pack, hunger-mad in the hush of the starlit night –
these are nothing compared with the thrills and the grip of aerial fight,
with the roar of the engine, the tang of the wires, the Vickers' stuttering rattle,
the shrieking and whooping, the mounting and swooping of rapidly flickering battle,
the swift-flung curves and the shuddering swerves, the turning, the twisting, the spinning
it is triumph and terror and frenzied delight to the end from the very beginning.
The joys of sailing in unknown waters and island-studded seas,
the feel of the boat as she forges along and heels to the touch of the breeze,
the sound of the ripples that gurgle and bubble, like fairy bells artfully tinkled,
the smell of the air and the touch on the face of the glittering spray, God-sprinkled,
the glory of snaking a frail canoe through a gap in the foam-swept crags
where the waters curl and eddy and swirl around the hidden snags,

the flurry and froth and the eager grip where the mighty tide is sweeping,
the paddle's whip at the well-timed stroke that sets the birch-bark leaping,
the pleasures of drifting on wooded lakes, shimmering, silent, and still,
with the blue of the sky and the pines nearby and the blue of the distant hill,
the cast and the quivering tenseness of muscle, the sudden fulfilment of wish,
the tug and the rapid bewildering tussle, the run of the well-hooked fish,
the leaps and the dives as he struggles and strives, the sickening dread and the rapture,
the slow, imperceptible gaining of hope and the ultimate glory of capture,
the victor's return through the silent wood with happiness rooted throughout him,
the sense of the glorious fitness of wonder in all that he sees about him,
these are splendid things to do, things for a man to love,
but not so good as the splendid things that a man may do up above.
The glory of gambolling high in the heavens in scenery weirdly entrancing,
abandoned and wholly free from restraint in the manner of primitive dancing,
the pleasure of being the absolute master of every turn and twist,
the feel of the craft as she spins about to every move of the wrist,
the satisfaction of doing each fling smooth and sure right through,
of knowing that every motion done is crisp and clean and true,
the joy of exploring fresh-found clouds, and hurtling down from the summit
in the swerving slide down the glacier side with the speed of a falling plummet
the power of taking the sky and the earth and making them do what he pleases,
the sight of places unblemished by man and the touch of untainted breezes,
the soothing noise and the graceful poise of soft and smooth descent,
the placid enjoyment of being alive and the feeling of utter content,
these are joys that none can better on earth or river or sea,
wheresoever and whatsoever his dreams of bliss may be.

Flight-Commander Jeffery Day, DSC, RNAS
1896-1918

William Butler Yeats, 1865-1939

An Irish Airman Foresees His Death
W B Yeats, 1918

Yeats, Irish poet and pillar of both the Irish and British 20th century literary establishments, was awarded the Nobel Prize for Literature in 1923 for "inspired poetry, which in a highly artistic form gives expression to the spirit of a whole nation".

He wrote this soliloquy in 1918. Not wishing to publish a political work which reflected the role of Irish soldiers fighting for Great Britain at a time of Irish nationalism, he delayed publication until 1919. It is widely believed that the airman was Major Robert Gregory, a friend of Yeats who died on the Piave front in Italy.

The poem has more intellectual and emotional than aviation content but has nevertheless become a favourite in aviation literature. It was cleverly woven into the script of the film *Memphis Belle*, the true story of a B-17 bomber's twenty-fifth, and last, bombing mission over Germany during World War II, before flying back to the U.S. to make a tour of the country in aid of the war effort. Take-off is delayed due to bad weather over the target and the crew are lying around on the grass of an English airfield, passing the time. One of them finds a note-book belonging to the waist gunner, Sergeant Danny Daly, a young (the average age of the whole crew was under 20) Irish-American. In it are scribblings of poetry, so his fellow crew-members tease him into quoting something that he has written. He quotes extracts from Yeats' poem. Only when the Flying Fortress is returning from its mission, badly shot-up, does Danny, lying in the fuselage, dreadfully wounded, confess that it was Yeats, and not he, who wrote it.

I know that I shall meet my fate
Somewhere among the clouds above;
Those that I fight I do not hate,
Those that I guard I do not love;
My country is Kiltartan Cross,
My countrymen Kiltartan's poor,
No likely end could bring them loss
Or leave them happier than before.

Nor law, nor duty bade me fight,
Nor public men, nor cheering crowds,
A lonely impulse of delight
Drove to this tumult in the clouds;
I balanced all, brought all to mind,
The years to come seemed waste of breath,
A waste of breath the years behind
In balance with this life, this death.

William Butler Yeats
1865-1939

The Pilot
Frederick Branford

Frederick Victor Branford was a Captain serving in 8 Squadron (Naval 8) of the Royal Naval Air Service during the First World War. On 1st March, 1917, during the battle of the Somme, he was flying a Sopwith Pup along the coast near the Zeeland town of Cadzanal when he engaged two German seaplanes, shooting one down. But he himself was shot down and badly wounded; he ditched his aircraft and swam ashore to Holland where he was interned.

Much of Branford's poetry was written during a long period of recovery from his injuries which left him totally disabled for the rest of his life.

This poem, which appeared in *Titan and Gods*, published in 1922, could serve as the epitaph for any RNAS pilot.

He is liege of wind and the thunder,
And desperate resolute things.
        On the market-skies
        His spirit buys
A drink of death on desolate wings.
        His hands
        Hold Fate
        He stands
        Like Hate
Between the winds and under
        The flashing brim
        Of the waters, slim
U-boats wilt at the sight of him.

He rides the wild cloud-horses
On tracks of polar gold.
        His heart is hound

Of the hunting-ground
Where the ghostly stags are foaled.
Through hives
Of stars,
He drives
His cars
Along moon-metalled courses
His feet are shod
With lightning rod,
To walk the living hand of God.

Captain Frederick Branford, RNAS
1892-1941

Night Flying
Frederick Branford

Aloft on footless levels of the night
A pilot thunders through the desolate stars
Sees in the misty deep a fainting light
Of far-off cities cast in coal-dark bars
Of shore and soundless sea; and he is lone,
Snatched from the universe like one forbid,
Or like a ghost caught from the slay and thrown
Out on the void, nor God cared what he did.

Till from these unlinked whisperers that pain
The buried earth he swings his boat away,
Even as a lonely thinker who has run
The gamut of great lore, and found the Inane,
Then stumbles at midnight upon a sun
And all the honour of a mighty day.

Captain Frederick Branford, RNAS
1892-1941

Gilbert Frankau, 1884-1952

Eyes in the Air
Gilbert Frankau

Jewish by birth, Gilbert Frankau was baptised as an Anglican. He was educated at Eton and went into the family cigar business until the out-break of the First World War when he became a Captain in the Royal Field Artillery. Invalided out, and the family business not having survived the war, he became a successful writer of novels and poetry for the rest of his life. His political ambitions failed as he was divorced three times – which was not acceptable to the Conservative Party of the time.

He wrote this poem in 1915 and first published it in *The Guns* in 1917.

Our guns are a league behind us, our target a mile below,
And there's never a cloud to blind us from the haunts of our lurking foe –
Sunk pit whence his shrapnel tore us, support-trench crest-concealed,
As clear as the charts before us, his ramparts lie revealed.
His panicked watchers spy us, a droning threat in the void;
Their whistling shells outfly us – puff upon puff, deployed
Across the green beneath us, across the flanking gray,
In fume and fire to sheathe us and baulk us of our prey.
Below, beyond, above her,
Their iron web is spun:
Flicked but unsnared we hover,
Edged planes against the sun;
Eyes in the air above his lair,
The hawks that guide the gun.

No word from earth may reach us, save, white against the
ground,
The strips outspread to teach us whose ears are deaf to sound:
But down the winds that sear us, athwart our engine's shriek,
We send – and know they hear us – the ranging guns we speak,
Our visored eyeballs show us their answering pennant, broke
Eight thousand feet below us, a whorl of flame-stabbed smoke –
The burst that hangs to guide us, while numbed gloved fingers
tap
From wireless key beside us the circles of the map.
Line – target – short or over –
Come, plain as clock hands run,
Unblinded; tail to sun;
Words out of air to range them fair,
From hawks that guide the gun.

Your flying shells have failed you, your landward guns are dumb:
Since earth hath nought availed you, these skies be open. Come,
Where, wild to meet and mate you, flame in their beaks for
breath,
Black doves, the white hawks wait you on the wind-tossed
boughs of death.
Those boughs be cold without you, our hearts are hot for this,
Our wings shall beat about you, our scorching breath shall kiss;
Till, fraught with what we gave you, fulfilled of our desire,
You bank – too late to save you from the biting beaks of fire –
Turn sideways from your lover,
Shudder and swerve and run,
Tilt; stagger; and plunge over
Doves dead in air, who clomb to dare
The hawks that guide the gun.

Gilbert Frankau
1884-1952

Two Pictures – 1917
Gordon Alchin

Gordon Alchin, like Gilbert Frankau, served in the Royal Field Artillery and then became a Captain in the Royal Flying Corps, being awarded the Air Force Cross. He paints a picture of a typical RFC aerodrome during the war.

Dawn…
And the dewy plain
Awakes to life and sound –
Where on the flying ground
The ghostly hangars blaze with lights again.
The giant birds of prey
Creep forth to a new day,
And one by one,
As morning gilds the dome,
Leave the grey aerodrome –
The day's begun.

Dusk…
And the vanish'd sun
Still streaks the evening skies;
Below, the prone earth lies
Darkened, wherever warring night has won.
The planes, returning, show
Deep black in the afterglow,
And one by one
Drop down from the higher airs,
– Down, down the invisible stairs –
The day is done.

Gordon Alchin, AFC, RFC
d.1947

A RNAS aircraft downed on the Belgian coast is protected by his escort from attack by a German seaplane
(Flight)

Reconnaisance
Gordon Alchin

It seems that Alchin, flying a routine reconnaissance sortie and enjoying the scenery, was 'bounced' by a single enemy aircraft.

I journeyed to the east,
Rolled on the surgent airs of autumn days:
Below, the earth lay creased
With myriad meadows in the morning haze.
Far off, where lay the sea,
A silvered mirror beckoned to my bent,
And, moving orderly,
The high cloud-armies marched magnificent.

Some menace in the sky,
Some quick alarm did wake me as I sped:
At once, unwarningly
Streamed out repeated death, from one that fled
Headlong before my turn –
But, unavoiding of the answering blast,
Checked sudden, fell astern –
And unmolested fared I to the last.

Gordon Alchin, AFC, RFC
d.1947

Aeroplanes
W J Turner

Walter James Redfern Turner was born in Melbourne in 1889 and came to England in 1907 to make a career for himself as a writer. From the First World War to the mid-1930s he was known primarily as a poet and WB Yeats gave him special attention in the 1936 *Oxford Book of Modern Verse*, saying that Turner's poetry left him "lost in admiration and astonishment". Turner died prematurely of a cerebral thrombosis.

Iron birds floating in the sky
  Prey remorselessly
On the tiny, obscure dot
  That is some great city,
Below, men-insects rend and tear,
  Women wring hands of pity.

I have flown a hundred miles
  Over the blurred plain,
Dropping devastation and death,
  Blotting men's nerves with pain –
Their miserable cries were as tiny as insects'
  Calling their God in vain.

The sounds of their oaths and lamentations
  Could not even reach up to me,
The clouds were at peace, no tribulation
  Disturbed the sky harmony,
Only my buzzing engine clanged
  And my heart beat dreadfully.

I laughed as I silently tossed blind Death
  Down on that insect people,
Dreadful it was in the peaceful sky
  To murder that insect people,
And never to hear a sound or cry
  Or a bell toll in a steeple.

I laughed when my last bloody bomb had gone,
  I shrieked high up in a cloud,
I wanted to fly in the face of their God
  And spit my disdain aloud,
I ripped through the terrified, whistling air
  And burst through the earth's damp shroud.

Ah! It was blue there, wide and clear,
  Dancing alive in the sun,
And millions of bright, sweet cymbals rang
  Praising the deeds I had done,
And millions of angels cheering stood
  Deep-columned around the Sun.

And then I stood erect and cheered,
  Ay! shouted into the sky,
I filled the vast semicircle round
  There was only the Sun and I,
The round, red, glittering, blazing Sun
  And a fluttering human fly.

W.J. Turner
1889-1946

William Henry Davies, 1871-1940

The Birds of Steel
William Henry Davies

William Henry Davies was a Welshman who, despite spending a significant part of his life as a Supertramp in the United States where he lost a leg trying to catch a moving train, was a prolific and popular poet. In 1926, he was awarded the degree of Doctor Litteris, honoris causa, from the University of Wales. In the citation for this award Professor Thomas described Davies as "... a man in whose work much of the peculiarly Welsh attitude to life is expressed with singular grace and sincerity... he has re-discovered for those who have forgotten them, the joys of simple nature... he is a lover of life... he affirms values that were falling into neglect, and in an age that is mercenary reminds us that we have the capacity for spiritual enjoyment." This poem, published in *Forty New Poems* in 1918, embodies those sentiments.

This apple-tree that once was green,
  Is now a thousand flowers in one!
And, with their bags strapped to their thighs
  There's many a bee comes for sweets,
To stretch every bag to its full size.

And when the night has grown a moon,
  And I lie half-asleep in bed,
I hear those bees again – ah no.
  It is the birds of steel, instead,
Seeking their innocent prey below.

Man-ridden birds of steel, unseen,
  That come to drop their murdering lime
On any child or harmless thing
  Before the early morning time:
Up, nearer to God, they fly and sing.

William Henry Davies
1871-1940

An early Norman Wilkinson painting of an RNAS Sopwith Batboat of the Dover Patrol.
Author's collection

The Joy of Flying
Paul Bewsher, France, 1917

When Paul Bewsher's book of poetry *The Dawn Patrol* was published in 1917, the Daily Graphic hailed the poet as being "the first airman-poet to regard humanity from the detached standpoint of the sky" and predicted that his book would "in after years be eagerly sought by collectors".

Bewsher was a pilot in the Royal Naval Air Service from 1915 to 1918. He was shot down and was awarded the Distinguished Service Cross. He subsequently transferred to the Royal Air Force where he served from 1918 to 1919.

I consider him, with Jeffery Day, both RNAS pilots, to have been the two leading pilot-poets of the First World War.

When heavy on my tired mind
  The world, and worldly things, do weigh,
And some sweet solace I would find,
  Into the sky I love to stray,
And, all alone, to wander round
In lone seclusion from the ground.

Ah! Then what solitude is mine –
  From grovelling mankind aloof!
Their road is but a thin-drawn line:
  Their busy house a scarce-seen roof.
That little stain of red and brown
They boast about! – It is their town!

How small their petty quarrels seem!
  Poor, crawling multitudes below;
Which, like the ants in feverous stream
  From place to place move to and fro!
Like ants they work: like ants they fight,
Assuming blindly they are right.

Soon their existence I forget,
  In joy that on these flashing wings
I cleave the skies – Oh! Let them fret –
  Now know I why the skylark sings
Untrammelled in the boundless air –
For mine it is his bliss to share!

Now do I mount a billowy cloud,
  Now do I sail low o'er a hill,
And with a seagull's skill endowed
  Circle, and wheel, and drop at will –
Above the villages asleep,
Above the valleys, shadowed deep,

Above the water-meadows green
  Whose streams, which intermingled flow,
Like silver lattice-work are seen
  A-gleam upon the plain below –
Above the woods, whose naked trees
Move new-born buds upon the breeze.

And far away above the haze
  I see white mountain-summits rise,
Whose snow with sunlight is ablaze
  And shines against the distant skies.
Such thoughts these towering ranges bring
That I float on a-wondering!

So do I love to travel on
  Through lonely skies, myself alone;
For then the feverish threat is gone
  Which on this earth I oft have known.
Kind is the God who lets me fly
In sweet seclusion through the sky!

Paul Bewsher, DSC, RNAS
1894-1966

The Dawn Patrol

Paul Bewsher, Luxeuil-les-Bains, 1917

Sometimes I fly at dawn above the sea,
Where, underneath, the restless waters flow –
  Silver, and cold, and slow.
Dim in the East there burns a new-born sun,
Whose rosy gleams along the ripples run,
  Save where the mist droops low,
Hiding the level loneliness from me.

And now appears beneath the milk-white haze
A little fleet of anchored ships, which lie
  In clustered company,
And seem as they are yet fast bound by sleep,
Although the day has long begun to peep,
  With red inflamed eye,
Along the still deserted ocean ways.

The fresh, cold wind of dawn blows on my face
As in the sun's raw heart I swiftly fly,
  And watch the seas glide by.
Scarce human seem I, moving through the skies,
And far removed from warlike enterprise-
  Like some great gull on high
Whose white and gleaming wings beat on through space.

Then do I feel with God, quite, quite alone,
High in the virgin morn, so white and still,
  And free from human ill.
My prayers transcend my feeble earth-bound plaints –
As though I sang among the happy Saints
  With many a holy thrill –
As though the glowing sun were God's bright Throne.

My flight is done. I cross the line of foam
That breaks around a town of grey and red,
  Whose streets and squares lie dead ahead
Beneath the silent dawn – then am I proud
That England's peace to guard I am allowed;–
  Then bow my humble head,
In thanks to Him who brought me safely home.

Paul Bewsher, DSC, RNAS
1894-1966

Flying at Dusk
Paul Bewsher

This tranquil poem, from *The Bombing of Bruges*, matches its subject.

There is no sun:
But in the West there glows
A sea of rose.
The day is done;
And slowly fades in robes of flaming light
Before the night,

Below me lies
A mist of deepest blue
Which stains the view
With sapphire dyes,
And all the countryside below is kissed
With dim blue mist.

Here in the sky,
I see the day is gone
And dusk creeps on;
And as I fly
I know that, for the first time, from the air,
The world looks fair.

Never before
Has beauty filled my eyes
From towering skies.
I never saw
Earth look romantic from the heights above,
But Dusk brings Love.

Paul Bewsher, DSC, RNAS
1894-1966

Nox Mortis
Paul Bewsher

The Afternoon
Flutters and dies:
The fairy moon
Burns in the skies
As they grow darker, and the first stars shine
On night's rich mantle – purple like warm wine.

On each white road
Begins to crawl
The heavy toad:
The night-birds call,
And round the trees the swift bats flit and wheel,
While from the barns the rats begin to steal.

So now must I,
Bird of the night
Toward the sky
Make wheeling flight,
And bear my poison o'er the gloomy land
And let it loose with hard unsparing hand.

The chafers boom
With whirring wings,
And haunt the gloom
Which twilight brings –
So in nocturnal travel do I wail
As through the night the wing-ed engines sail.

Death, Grief and Pain
Are what I give,
O that the slain
Might live – might live!
I know them not for I have blindly killed,
And nameless hearts with nameless sorrow filled.

Thrice curs-ed War
Which bids that I
Such death should pour
Down from the sky.
O, Star of peace, rise swiftly in the East
That from such slaying men may be released.

Paul Bewsher, DSC, RNAS
1894-1966

A Night Ascent
A British night-flying biplane leaving in the light of a ground flare
(Flight)

Searchlights
Paul Bewsher

You who have seen across the star-decked skies
The long white arms of searchlights slowly sweep
Have you imagined what it is to creep
High in the darkness, cold and terror-wise,
For ever looked for by those cruel eyes
Which search with far-flung beams the shadowy deep,
And near the wings unending vigil keep
To haunt the lonely airman as he flies?

Have you imagined what it is to know
That if one finds you, all their fierce desire
To see you fall will dog you as you go,
High in a sea of light and bursting fire,
Like some small bird, lit up and blinding white
Which slowly moves across the shell-torn night?

Paul Bewsher, DSC, RNAS
1894-1966

The Night Raid
Paul Bewsher, France, 1917

This is not only a fine description of night flying but also the thoughts that go through the pilot's mind, conscious of the indiscriminate damage that he must cause below.

Around me broods the dim, mysterious Night,
Star-lit and still.
No whisper comes across the Plain,
Asleep beneath the breezes light,
Which scarcely stir the growing grain.
Slow chimes the quiet midnight hour
In some unseen and distant tower,
While round me broods the vague, mysterious Night,
Star-lit, and cool, and still.

And I must desecrate this silent time
Of drowsy dreams!
On mighty wings towards the sky,
Towards the stars, I have to climb
And o'er the sleeping country fly,
And such far-echoing clamour make
That all the villages must wake.
So must I desecrate this quiet time
Of soft and drowsy dreams!

The hour comes...soon must I say farewell
To this fair earth.
Then to my little room I go
Where I perhaps no more shall dwell.
Shall I return? – The Gods but know.
Perchance again I shall not sleep
On that white bed in silence deep.
For soon the hour comes to say farewell
To this fair, friendly earth.

I stand there long, before into the gloom
I take my way.
There are the pictures of my friends
And all the treasures of my room
On which my lamp soft radiance sends.
And long with lingering gaze I look
Upon each much beloved book.
I stand, and dream – before into the gloom
I sadly take my way.

And now I gain the field whence I must part
Upon my quest.
My Pegasus of wood and steel
Is ready straining at the start.
The governor is at the wheel –
And, with an ever-growing roar,
Across the hidden fields we soar.
So, with one envious look from Earth I part
Upon my midnight quest.

Beneath me lies the sleeping countryside
Hazy and dim,
And here and there a little gleam,
Like stars upon the heavens wide,
Speaks of some wretch who cannot dream –
But on his bed all night must toss
And hear me as I pass across,
In droning flight above the countryside,
Hazy, and huge, and dim.

And in the great blue night I ever rise
Towards the stars,
As to the hostile lands I sail
High in the dark and cloudless skies
Whose gloom our gloomy wings doth veil.
Beneath, a scarce-seen ribbon shows
Where through the woods a river flows,
As in the shadowy night I ever rise
Towards the scattered stars.

Now high above War's frontiers do I sit –
 Above the lines.
Great lights, like flowers, rise and fall:
On either side red flashes spit
Hot death at those poor souls which crawl
On secret errands, O, how grim
Must be that midnight slaughter dim!
And happy am I that so high I sit
 Above those cruel lines!

Each man beneath me now detests my race
 With iron hate.
Each tiny light I see must shine
Upon some grim, unfriendly face,
Who curses England's name and mine,
And would be glad if both were gone –
But steadily must I fly on,
Though every soul beneath me loathes my race
 With stern, unceasing hate.

I see a far-flung City all ablaze
 With jewelled lamps:
I trace its quays, its roads, its squares,
And all its intermingled ways,
And, as I wonder how it dares
To flaunt itself, – the City dies,
And in an utter darkness lies,
For I have terrified that town ablaze
 With twinkling, jewelled lamps.

But, see! – the furnace with its ruddy breath
 Which I must wreck!
The searchlights sweep across the sky –
Long-fingered ministers of Death –
I look deep in their cold blue eye,
Incessant shells with blinding light
Show every wire, clear and white!
There is the furnace with its ruddy breath
 Which I must wreck; -

It lies beneath – my time has come at last
            To do my work!
I wait – O! will you never stop
Your fearful shells, that burst so fast? –
And then – I hear destruction drop
Behind my back as I release
Such fearful death with such great ease.
Burst on, you shells! My time has come at last
            To do my deadly work.

Then do I turn, and hurry swiftly back
            Towards my home.
I gladly leave that place behind!
No more I hear the shrapnel's crack –
No more my eyes the searchlights blind.
I cross the lines with lightening breast
And sail into the friendly West.
How glad am I to hurry swiftly back
            Towards my peaceful home!

I reach the field – and then I softly land.
            My work is o'er!
I leave my hot and panting steed,
And clasp a comrade's outstretched hand,
And with him to my bedroom speed.
Then, over steaming beakers set,
The night's fierce menace soon forget.
How great a welcome waits me when I land –
            When all my work is o'er!

But ere I search shy sleep on my white bed
            I greet the dawn,
And think, with heart weighed down with grief,
How cruel this dawn to those whose dead
Lie shattered, torn – whom, like a thief
At darkest midnight, I have slain.
Poor, unknown victims! – real my pain!
What widows, orphans, sweethearts see their dead
            This cruel, hopeless dawn?

Paul Bewsher, DSC, RNAS
1894-1966

The Horrors of Flying
Paul Bewsher, France, 1917

From *The Joy of Flying* to *The Horrors of Flying* probably encompasses several months of operational sorties, many of them at night over enemy territory, and describes well the transition from the pilot's initial enthusiasm to see combat to that weariness, disillusionment and increasing fear of being shot down that most pilots suffered as the war progressed. Although Bewsher was eventually shot down he survived and lived to the age of 72.

The day is cold; the wind is strong;
And through the sky great cloud-banks throng,
While swathes of snow lie on the ground
O'er which I walk without a sound,
But I have vowed to fly today
Though winds are fierce and clouds are grey.
My aeroplane is on the field;
So I must fly – my fate is sealed,
And no excuses can I make;
Within its back my place I take,
I strap myself inside the seat
And press the rudder with my feet,
And hold the wheel with nervous grip
And gaze around my little ship –
For on its wire-rigging taught
Depends my life – which will be short
If it should fail me in the air;
Swift then my fall, and short my prayer,
And these my wings would be my pyre –
So well I scrutinise each wire!
Then out across the field I go
In shaking progress, – noisy – slow;
And turn, until the wind I face,

Then do I look around a space;
For fear today is at my heart
And nervously I fear to start.
The field is clear – the skies are bare –
Mine is the freedom of the air!
And yet I sit and hesitate,
Although each moment that I wait
Brings to my soul a greater fear.
To me the grass seems very dear –
Dear seems the hut where dreams have crept
To me each midnight as I slept –
Dear seems the river, by whose brink
I oft have watched brown pebbles sink
Deep in the crumbling bridge's shade,
Where in the evening I have strayed!
My restless hands hold fast the wheel;
Once more the wing-controls I feel.
I move the rudder with my feet,
And settle firmly in the seat.
I start, and o'er the snowy grass
In ever quicker progress pass:
On either side the ground streaks by,
And soon above the grass I fly.
I feel the air beneath the wings;
At first a greater ease it brings –
But soon the stormy strife begins,
And if I lose,'tis Death who wins.
The winds a thousand devils hold,
Who grasp my wings with fingers bold,
And keep me ceaselessly a-rock–
I seem to hear those devils mock
As I am thrown from side to side
In unseen eddies, terrified –
As suddenly I start to drop,
And when my plunging fall I stop,
Up am I swiftly thrown once more!
Like no great eagle do I soar,

But like a sparrow tempest-tost
I struggle on! My faith is lost:
My former confidence is dead,
And whispering fear has come instead.
Death ever dogs me close behind –
My frightened soul no peace can find.
I feel a torture in each nerve,
As to the right or left I swerve.
And now Imagination brings
Its evil thoughts – I watch the wings,
And wonder if those wings will break –
The tight-stretched wires seem to shake.
I see the ghastly headlong rush,
And picture how the fall would crush
My helpless body on the ground.
With haggard eyes I turn around,
And contemplate the rocking tail, –
My drawn and sweating cheeks are pale.
Fear's clammy hands clutch at my heart!
I try, with unavailing art,
To summon thoughts of peaceful hours
Spent in some sunny field of flowers
When my half-opened eyes would look
On some old dream-inspiring book,
And not on this accursed wheel,
And on this box of wood and steel
At which at pitch and toss with Death,
I play, and wonder if each breath
I tensely draw will be my last.
The happy thoughts are swiftly past –
My frightened brain forbids them stay.
Dear London seems so far away,
And far away my well-loved friends!
Each second my existence ends
In my disordered mind, whose pace
I cannot check – its cog-wheels race,
Like some ungoverned whirring clock,

When, frenziedly, it runs amok.
I have resolved that I will climb
A certain height – how slow seems time
As on its sluggish pivot creeps
The laggard finger-point, which keeps
The truthful record. O, how slow
Towards the clouds I seem to go!
And then ambition gains its mark at last!
The little finger o'er the point has passed!
I can descend again. With conscience clear
And end this battle with persistent fear!
The engine's clamour dies – there is no sound
Save whistling wires – as toward the ground
I gently float. My agony is gone.
What peace is mine as I go gliding on!
Calm after storm – contentment after pain –
Soft sleep to some tempestuous, burning brain –
The soothing harbour after foamy seas –
The gentle feeling of a perfect ease –
All, all are mine – though yet by gusts distressed!
Near is the ground, and with the ground comes rest.
Above the trees I glide – above the grass,
Above the snow-besprinkled earth I pass.
I touch the ground, run swift along, and stop –
Above the wheel my tired shoulders drop.
I leave my seat and slowly move away…
Cold is the wind: the clouds are grey,
I only wish my room to gain,
And in some book forget my pain,
And lose myself in fancied dreams
Across Titania's golden streams.

Paul Bewsher, DSC, RNAS
1894 – 1966

The Aeroplane (Part III)
Arthur Vine Hall

The Reverend Arthur Vine Hall was a South African. This is Part III of his poem *The Aeroplane* from his book *The Submarine and the Aeroplane*, published shortly after the First World War. In it he picks up on Tennyson's 1842 predictions, in *Locksley Hall*, of aviation, aerial warfare and the United Nations, and laments Man's continued inability to cease from warfare. As an example of the chivalry that still existed during the late war he tells how a pilot of the Royal Flying Corps dropped a wreath on the grave of Max Immelman, the German fighter ace who was greatly respected by the British pilots. A wreath was similarly dropped in memory of Oswald Boelke.

Although I have used Tennyson's poem in the section Prophecies and Aspirations I repeat it here for ease of reference before reading Vine Hall's poem.

Locksley Hall (extract)

Men, my brothers, men the workers, ever reaping
something new:
That which they have done but earnest of the things that
they shall do:
For I dipped into the future, far as human eye could see,
Saw the vision of the world, and all the wonder that would
be;
Saw the heavens fill with commerce, argosies of magic
sails,
Pilots of the purple twilight, dropping down with costly
bales;
Heard the heavens fill with shouting, and there rained a
ghastly dew

From the nations' airy navies grappling in the central blue;
Far along the world wide whisper of the south-wind
rushing warm
With the standards of the peoples plunging through the
thunder-storm;
Till the war-drum throbbed no longer, and the battle flag
was furled
In the Parliament of man, the Federation of the world.

The Aeroplane

Poet, who dreamed of dreadful dew
From airy navies in the blue
Grappling, and heard the heavens fill
With shouting nations mad to kill, –
These eighty years have brought to birth
Those sounding heavens, that ghastly earth!
On sea and desolated shore
Romance of battle is no more.
War has become a devilish thing
Whence Chivalry has taken wing,
And wrathful at what is daily done,
Climbs the great spaces of the sun.
There, wing to wing and face to face,
War's ancient courtesies have place.
We think of how, towards the grave
Of Immelmann, an airman dave.
Blossoms of death about him broke,
Shedding their petals of white smoke, –
A lurking asp in every rose!
Yet flying down among his foes,
Bullets around, above, beneath,
He dropped upon the grave a wreath.
O Prophet of the ghastly dew!
When will that other word come true?
And the heavens fill with magic sails –

Fair argosies with costly bales,
That through the purple twilight glide
Adown an ever bloodless tide?
When will the battle flags be furled? –
A "Parliament of man": a world
Wherein the love of love is born,
"The hate of hate, the scorn of scorn"?
  When? When the unutterable guilt
Of all the blood profanely spilt
Since the first brother lay there – slain
By the first of this red, red race of Cain;
When all the grief of all the years,
To this last agony of tears –
This self-made misery of man –
Has taught us (if it ever can!)
No more to worship but abhor
The murderous Antichrist of War.
  O ye, the Wise, the Good, the Great!
Pouring for this fell Lord of Hate
Libations such as these; who praise
Him in your Art, your Song; who raise
For him such temples; shower your gold
For him – the uncrucified, unsold;
Who bid your herald angels sing:
"Barabbas is our chosen king!" –
Hearken before it be too late.
Millions are surging at your gate!
One word alone their wrath can quell;
Back, back, vile devil! – back to Hell!
Take Thou, O Christ, Thy rightful place:
Return, restore a ruined race.

Arthur Vine Hall

The Dying Aviator
Anonymous

This little ditty was sung, no doubt with gusto, by RFC pilots to the tune of *My Bonny Lies over the Ocean*, by strange coincidence the same tune to which later Fleet Air Arm pilots sang *The Stringbag Song* (see p.247). Although it can only qualify as doggerel, I include it because it captures the spirit of the young men who, with scant experience and much bravery, went to war in the early fighting aircraft. There are many variations from both World Wars so I have chosen the lines and verses that I think give a reasonably sensible and amusing version which also scans!

The bold aviator lay dying,
And while 'neath the wreckage he lay (he lay),
To the sobbing mechanics around him,
These last dying words he did say.

"Take the piston rings out of my stomach,
And the cylinders out of my brain (my brain).
From the seat of my pants take the crankshaft,
And assemble the engine again."

"Take the manifold out of my larynx,
And the butterfly valve off my neck (my neck).
Remove from my kidneys the conrods,
There's a lot of good parts in this wreck."

"Pull the longeron out of my backbone,
The turnbuckle out of my ear (my ear),
From the small of my back take the rudder –
There's all of your aeroplane here."

"I'll be riding a cloud in the morning,
With no rotary engine to cuss (to cuss).
Take the lead from your feet and get busy,
There's another lad needing the bus."

Anonymous

The Golden Age
1918-1939

Introduction

The end of the First World War in 1918 heralded what is universally known as the Golden Age of Aviation which filled the inter-war years and was so-called because of the great developments made in all aspects of flight during the years that the world was at peace.

The First World War had given huge impetus to aircraft and engine design and whereas there was considerable danger of both airframe and engine failure at the outset, by the end of the war both had achieved a significantly greater standard of reliability. What was of huge benefit to aspiring aviators was the number of war surplus aeroplanes that could be purchased cheaply, thus spawning the 'barnstormers', mostly young pilots for whom flying had become an essential part of their lives, and who travelled America and Britain bringing the aeroplane to the public with their air-shows.

A great impetus came from the postal services. As soon as reliability of delivery became a fact, internal postal air services sprung up all over the world, to be shortly followed by international services as soon as airfields had been prepared and long range aeroplanes delivered. For aerial post to be a success, the aeroplanes and their crews had to be able to deliver on a daily basis, whatever weather or other obstructions stood in the way, and casualties were correspondingly high.

With the barnstormers and the postal pilots came the adventurers. Speed was the main driver in an age when surface travel by road, rail and sea took weeks and months. The aeroplane reduced these trips to days and hours. So as soon as the landing grounds were cleared – often only grass clearings in virgin country – adventurous men and women set out, initially to prove that travel by air was a practical prospect and then to make ever faster flights as the aircraft industries of the world produced better and more reliable machines. Point-to-point records were established all over the world with the routes between capital cities – London to Paris, New York to San Francisco, Paris to Dakar – providing the pilots with challenges and fame.

Finally the oceans were conquered. With no prospect of making a forced landing in some open field, the airframe and engine had to promise long hours of reliability for the first trans-ocean flights. Pilots such as Alcock and Brown, Lindbergh, Earhart and Kingsford Smith, all became household names as they conquered one ocean after another, first as crews and then as solo flyers.

The British Empire gave great impetus to the nation's aviation. Linking London with Cape Town, Bombay, Montreal, Singapore and Sydney had hitherto been accomplished only by long sea voyages. Now the air promised to bring the dominions, colonies and protectorates ever closer to the mother country.

The poetry ceased to reflect the novelty of aviation and while successive flyers still marvelled at the spectacular images of cloud and landscape, seen by them for the first time, more was written about the social consequences of air travel and aerial adventure and inevitably, as another world conflict loomed, the development of the fighting machines preparing for another world war.

The Airman Demobbed
Cuthbert Hicks

All four of Cuthbert Hicks's poems appeared in Stella Wolfe Murray's anthology *The Poetry of Flight* published in 1925. They reflect the poet's recent life in the RAF and demobilisation at the end of the First World War. Sadly I can find little about the author other than, after demobilisation, he moved to the United States where he became a journalist.

I rode on the storm and the lightning
And raced the gay clouds as I flew,
Dipped under the arch of the rainbow,
And swung like a star in the blue.

I slid down the path of the sunbeams,
And swooped like a gull to the wave
I dropped o'er the crest of the mountains,
Down the streams that the valleys gave.

Now my feet are leaden and earthbound,
And I know why the caged bird dies,
For my soul leaps out to the blue ways,
When I dare look up at the skies.

Cuthbert Hicks

Per Ardua ad Astra
Cuthbert Hicks

On the morning of 19th February, 1919, a memorial service for members of the Royal Air Force was held in Westminster Abbey. It inspired Cuthbert Hicks to write this poem.

For Life is Flight and Death is Flight
And the Pilot takes his due.

How could I know, since for all time,
Lonely I swept upon the great blue ways,
And bore on my old wings the souls of men,
From dull earth to the starry maze.

I watched you wing uncharted space
Too young to learn the mysteries of God,
And so I snatched you swiftly, and I laid
Your young limbs glory in the sod.

But now my burden shall you share,
And your young wings I'll teach the way to keep.
That points the pathway to the sun, and send
All evil spinning to the deep.

For when you flash out on patrol,
'Tis you shall guide all tired souls to rise
Up to the happy landing grounds of God,
My spirit squadrons of the skies.

For Life is Flight and Death is Flight,
And the Pilot takes his due.

Cuthbert Hicks

In Memoriam, RAF
Cuthbert Hicks

This short poem must have been written as a tribute to the RNAS, RFC and RAF pilots killed during the First World War.

It is not long ago you skyward leapt
With joy into the radiance of the blue,
Perhaps you sought the hiding-place of stars,
And wistful leaned towards the limitless.

Perhaps on high the unseen glamour called,
And wings invisible supported you,
For I believe the hand of God stretched down
And lifted up your soul to the beyond.

You broke the barriers that keep all men
A little lower than the angels are,
You have migrated, but you will return,
And bring a message from the eyes that see.

Cuthbert Hicks

The Blind Man Flies
Cuthbert Hicks

For reasons that I give later in my introduction to Magee's *High Flight* there can be no doubt that this poem had some influence on the young Royal Canadian Air Force pilot's famous sonnet.

I am blind, I have never seen
Sun, gold nor silver moon,
Nor the fairy faces of flowers,
Nor the radiant moon.

They speak of the dawn and the dusk,
And the smile of a child,
Of the deep red heart of a rose,
As of God undefiled.

But I learnt from the air today
(On a bird's wings I flew),
That the earth could never contain
All of the God I knew.

I felt the blue mantle of space,
And kissed the cloud's white hem,
I heard the stars majestic choir,
And sang my praise with them.

Now joy is mine through my long night,
I do not feel the rod,
For I have danced the streets of heaven,
And touched the face of God.

Cuthbert Hicks

A Little Prayer for the Man in the Air
John Oxenham

John Oxenham was one of the pen names used by William Arthur Dunkerley when he wrote poetry, hymns and novels. Born in 1852 he was a prolific writer and served as deacon and teacher at the Ealing Congregational Church from the 1880s, later moving to Worthing where he became the town's mayor. It is likely that he had little more than a passing interest in aviation and that the inspiration for his poem stemmed more from his religious calling.

I never hear
The growling diapason of a plane
Up there,
The deep reverb'rant humming of a plane
Up there,
But up to God I wing a little prayer,
Begging His care
For him who braves the dangers of the air.

"God keep you, Bird-man, in your plane
Up there!
Your wings upbear, your heart sustain!
Give you good flight and oversight,
And bring you safe to earth again!"

I, too, have hostages with fortunes up above,
And what may come to you may come to mine,
So, once again, – "God speed you as you rove!
Both you and mine to His care I consign."

John Oxenham (William Arthur Dunkerley)
1852-1941

Initiation
E Vine Hall

This poem taken from *In Full Flight*, and published in 1921 by A and F Denny Ltd., 147 Strand, London WC2, cost 3s 6d (17½p), but try as I might I cannot find a copy. *Initiation* constitutes another fine tribute to the aviators of the Golden Age.

What was the relationship between Arthur Vine Hall and E. Vine Hall?

That I have lived to see men fly
In remote reaches of the sky,
Ready the darkest hour to dare
In the deep spaces of the air,
To take their station by the stars,
And to stand sentry at the bars
Of sunset: to excel in speed
The very vulture, to exceed
For height the hawk, for grace the gull,
Man's marks and limits to annul,
Till earth shrink to an island, hung
The heaven's other orbs among,
And the world but a shadow seems
Of unintelligible dreams,
Staggers my soul. Therefore I see,
As knit in one society,
Seers, saints and airmen; all who rise
To the pure place of the clear skies
And read, as in a mirror's face,
The hidden things of time and space.

E Vine Hall

The Liberty Motor
Henry W King

It is difficult to write poetically about machinery. Rudyard Kipling succeeded brilliantly in *MacAndrew's Hymn*, describing, in the words of a Scots Chief Engineer, the workings of a marine steam engine.

Henry King writes more romantically about the Liberty motor, a US aero engine produced at the end of World War I. The design and production of these engines is a splendid example of American industry at its best. The engine, of which there were 4, 6, 8 and 12 cylinder versions, was designed in five days by Jesse Vincent and E J Hall, confined to the Willard Hotel in Washington in May, 1917 for the purpose. By the fall of 1917 the US War Department had placed an order for 22,500 of the 12 cylinder version, to be built as quickly as possible by the US automobile and engine manufacturers Buick, Ford, Lincoln, Packard and others. Ford built all 433,826 cylinders for these engines and by the end of the First World War production was at the rate of 150 engines a day.

Silent, she rests before the sweeping wing
Bound fast to tautened wires and straining spars,
Which she will swing aloft till heaven bars
Her progress. She a steel and iron Thing?
Ah, no – ye never heard the goddess sing
As she whirled headlong towards the dizzy stars,
Chanting her love-song for the god of wars;
Fierce love of him when all her metals ring.

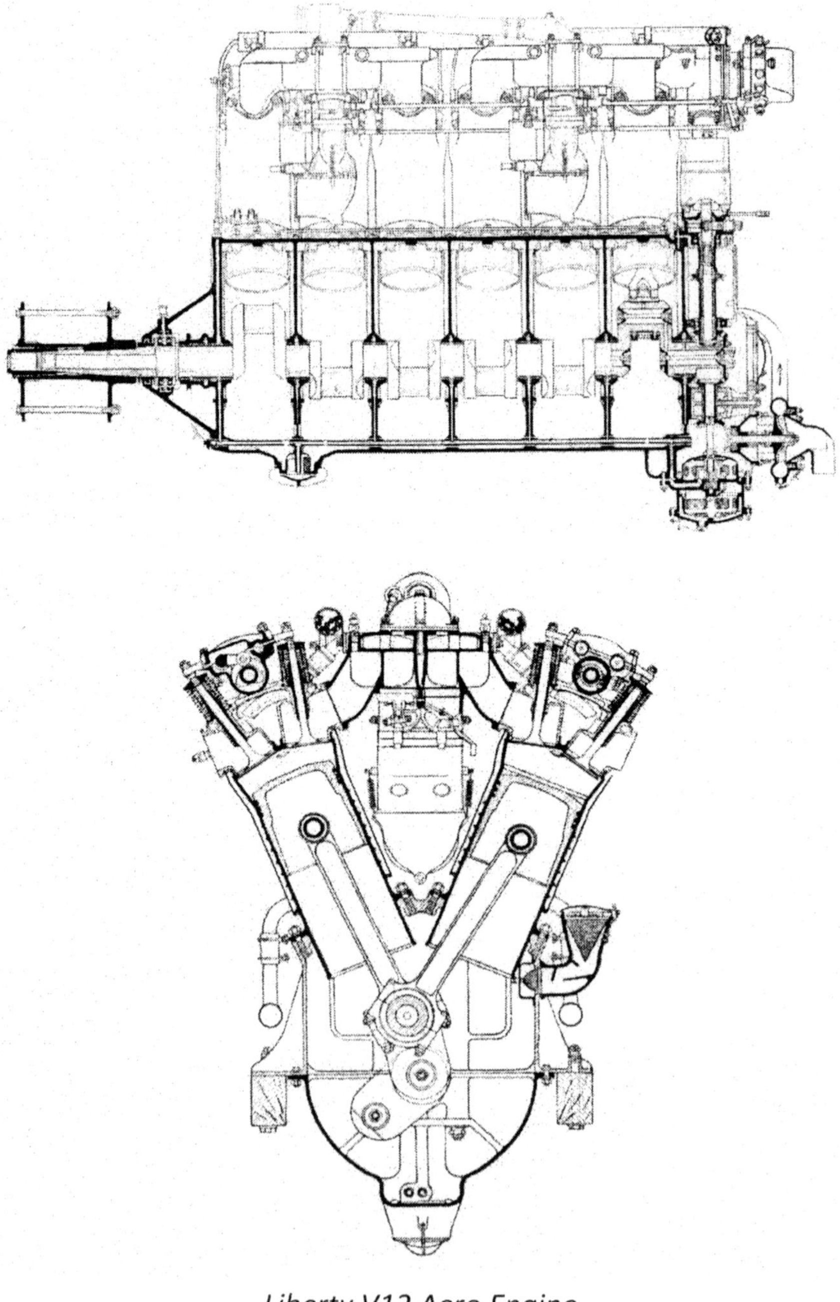

Liberty V12 Aero Engine

Her very heart is made of steel and fire,
Her panting breaths are drawn with countless gears.
No less the burden of her fierce desire
Makes swelling music in a freeman's ears.
For, though the scientist has been her sire,
He knows she was half-born of women's tears.

Henry W King

Trailmen of the Air
Arthur Chapman

Born in 1873 in Rockford, Illinois, Arthur Chapman became a reporter, first in Chicago and then in Denver, Colorado. He is best known for his writings about the West, particularly his poem *Out Where The West Begins*, which was considered the best known poem in America during the 1920s and 1930s. The advent of the aeroplane obviously did little to dispel his nostalgia for the traditional ways of the West.

Over the pines, where we used to go under,
And the world all white below,
With the eagle watching our flight with wonder,
On the lawbreaker's trail we go,
Thief of a Cree, with a sledful of takings,
Frenchy, who murdered a pard;
They and their kind are our combings and rakings –
Since the airplane crew stands guard.

Over the plains where we plodded long hours,
To the squeak of the snowshoe thongs,
Now we look down, as from sky-piercing towers,
While the motor is droning its song,
Weary the miles we made in the saddle,
Short are those miles today;
And yet for the pony, the sled and the paddle
We long as we wing our way.

Arthur Chapman
1873-1935

The Song of the Bird Man
Roselle Mercier Montgomery

Considered Georgia's best, and one of America's finest poetesses, Roselle Mercier was born in 1874. She married a distinguished New York lawyer, J Seymour Montgomery, and lived in Connecticut until her untimely death in 1933. She was best known for her *Ulysses Returns* and several quotations, a favourite of which was "Never a ship sails out of the bay but carries my heart as a stowaway". I do wonder whether the word 'wings' in the last line of the third verse should not be 'winds', but cannot find an original version of the poem to prove it.

Brother am I to the flying things –
As up I mount on my flashing wings
That lift and soar as my motor sings!

Voyager of the blue am I,
Traveller of the trackless sky –
Yes, I am one with the things that fly!

Daedalus, Icarus, live in me –
All who dreamed of the wings to be –
Joy with me when the wings blow free!

Joy of the hovering gulls I know
When restless waters lie green below,
And great swift ships to my wings seem slow!

Joy of the soaring eagle is mine,
When mountains fade to a dim blue line,
As high I soar in the clear sunshine!

Like silver ribbons the rivers gleam,
Like checker-boards do the valleys seem –
Earth, with its cares, like a vanished dream!

Beneath me man and his works seem small!
City towers – I top them all!
Like ants, below me, the earth-bound crawl:

How can they know, poor creeping things,
Gladness of living that flying brings,
Madness of motion – the joy of wings!

Scarce can I see them, the pygmies there,
Who have never learned to dream and dare,
And I thank my God as I mount the air!

Life? It is mine in the ether clear,
Love? Let it wait – I will have no fear,
Death? Let it come – I will meet it here!

Roselle Mercier Montgomery
1874-1933

The Army of the Planes
Minna Irving

The alliteration and onomatopoeia of this poem invoke images of the Thousand Bomber raids of World War II and warrant a place in any aviation anthology.

Minna Irving, was born, lived and died in Tarrytown, New York. She was a prolific writer from the age of 15 and was known nationally for her patriotic wartime poetry. Twice married, she was a well-known character in Tarrytown where she walked daily, with her mother four steps behind her, to the post office "accessorised with a huge hat, whatever the season, to go along with her tailored gowns, shoes and parasols. She wore two rings on each of her eight fingers, ranging from diamonds and emeralds to sapphires and opals". Her poetry was as colourful and dramatic as she herself.

They are coming with the drumming of a million pinions
  humming
And the purr of mighty motors that are all in time and
  tune.
Proudly soaring with the roaring of a thousand northers
  pouring
Through the vast and hollow spaces sacred to the sun and
  moon.
They are racing into places with radiant star faces,
Following the meteor's speedways and the comet's ancient
  lanes,
And the universe is shaking and the waking earth is
  quaking
At the terror and the marvel of the army of the planes.
Wings of wonder as they thunder sweep the rolling clouds
  asunder,

Sailing great uncharted oceans of the empyrean blue;
Struts are singing, wires are ringing, swift propeller blades are flinging
Spray of diamond dust and silver when they cut a star in two.
Hail the aerial squadrons forming, through the fields of azure storming,
Battle birds the crimson war god to celestial combat trains,
Swooping down from viewless regions to the aid of earthly legions –
Hail the glorious, victorious, valiant army of the planes!

Minna Irving
1865-1940

The Desert Mail (Cairo – Baghdad, 1922)
J.O.P.E.

I have failed to discover who JOPE was but his poem appears in Stella Wolfe Murray's anthology *The Poetry of Flight*, having originally been printed in *The Aeroplane*, the other British weekly aviation magazine. In the interwar years Britain's influence in the Middle East was dominant and the Royal Air Force, because of the distances involved, was given the responsibility for keeping the peace, which it did very effectively with a couple of squadrons of aircraft and some armoured cars. Mail delivery by air was also one of it's duties and this poem describes the long haul involved between Egypt and Iraq. My calculator makes the actual distance between Cairo and Baghdad to be 805 statute miles or 698 nautical miles, so the poet must have flown the first two hundred before the start of the poem!

Clean cut against the first faint flush of dawn,
  Their silver planes outstretched to catch the sun,
Hastening to meet the Day as yet unborn,
  Faint upon the earth their engines' muted hum.
Below – the Desert lies in shadows dim,
  A vast, inverted bowl of yellow sand.
The distant hills, eternal guardians grim,
  Flaking the entrance to a barren land.

For His Majesty's Mails are travelling East,
  (Mark the Track as it winds below.)
His Majesty's Mails are travelling East,
  (Six hundred weary miles to go!)

The ashes of a fire – lit all in vain –
 A Thing that lived and breathed but yesterday,
The charred and blackened wreckage of a 'plane,
 Are all that mark the Man Who Lost his Way.
An error of a minute; a side-slip in a cloud;
 He failed to see the Track he thought he knew,
Then endless days of waiting – by fear and hunger cowed –
 Ere the jackals took the meat that was their due!

For His Majesty's Mails are travelling East,
 (The Track is dim in the sand below.)
His Majesty's Mails are travelling East.
 (Only two hundred miles to go!)

In the bitter cold of Winter, when the sullen engines fret,
 And the leaden sky above them bids them stay,
In the storm or in the sunshine; in the dry or in the wet,
 The Air Mail passes swiftly on its way.
In the hottest days of Summer, when the water-holes are
 dry,
 And the Desert's full of things that are not there,
The gaunt and weary jackal sees the shadows passing by
 Of the Mail 'planes as they hurry through the air.

For His Majesty's Mails are travelling East,
(The Arrow is pointing the way to go,)
His Majesty's Mails are travelling East,
(Those are the Bitumen Pools below.)

We have placed at your disposal all the arts we learnt in War,
And for ninepence you can purchase, if you're wise,
The same efficient service of the Man who Yesterday,
Chased the black-crossed Birds of War from out your skies.
The letters that they carry from Cairo to the East,
Bear little slips of paper, coloured blue,
And the loss of crew and pilot doesn't matter in the least,
If the Mail Bags see the Desert journey through!

For His Majesty's Mails are travelling East.
(The Track is lost but the way we know.)
His Majesty's Mails are travelling East.
(Baghdad City to port below!)

J.O.P.E.

Air Commodore (then Group Captain) Sir Nigel Norman, RAF
(by kind permission of Sir Torquil Norman)

First Solo
Nigel Norman

Nigel Norman had served in the Royal Artillery during the First World War and afterwards he went up to Cambridge to read engineering and architecture, graduating in 1922. He learned to fly at Stag Lane in 1926 and from that time until his untimely death in 1943, aviation was central to his life.

I want to be a windfarer, to climb
  On hidden waves, through airy wastes, to share
The mystery and the mastery of the air,
  My generation's secret from all time.

How few men yet have known that power sublime;
  Mere thousands! Led by that great few, whose care,
Whose courage, nay! whose lives went, to prepare
  That ocean highway more than maritime!

Great Pioneers! When, the first time, I fare
  Out on those new-found seas of yours alone,
Let me salute you! This shall be my prayer:
  "Oh God, I thank thee that I, too, have flown!"

Air Commodore Sir Nigel Norman, RAF
1897-1943

"All the News That's Fit to Print."

The New York Times.

LINDBERGH DOES IT! TO PARIS IN 33½ HOURS; FLIES 1,000 MILES THROUGH SNOW AND SLEET; CHEERING FRENCH CARRY HIM OFF FIELD

COULD HAVE GONE 500 MILES FARTHER

Gasoline for at Least That Much More Flew at Times From 10 Feet to 10,000 Feet Above Water.

ATE ONLY ONE AND A HALF OF HIS FIVE SANDWICHES

Fell Asleep at Times but Quickly Awoke—Glimpses of His Adventure in Brief Interview at the Embassy

LINDBERGH'S OWN STORY TOMORROW

CROWD ROARS THUNDEROUS WELCOME

Breaks Through Lines of Soldiers and Police and Surging to Plane Lifts Weary Flier from His Cockpit

AVIATORS RESCUE HIM FROM FRENZIED MOB OF 25,000

Paris Boulevards Ring With Celebration After Day and Night Watch—American Flag Is Called For and Widly Acclaimed.

LEVINE ABANDONS BELLANCA FLIGHT

LINDBERGH TRIUMPH THRILLS COOLIDGE

New York Stages Big Celebration After Hours of Anxious Waiting

The New York Times announces Lindbergh's record solo flight of 20th/21st May, 1927

Science, Freedom, Beauty, Adventure
Charles A Lindbergh

In 1927 Charles Augustus Lindbergh, achieved enduring fame by making the first solo non-stop crossing of the Atlantic in his Ryan monoplane, *Spirit of St Louis*. Throughout his life he was a controversial man, principally because of his opposition to American involvement in World War II which only ceased with the Japanese attack on Pearl Harbour. Despite earlier service in the US Army Air Corps his re-enlistment was refused, but he nevertheless flew 50 combat missions as a civilian P-38 Lightning pilot in the Pacific. After the war he withdrew from public attention but maintained extensive aviation interests. On his death in 1974 he left almost 3,000 pages of writing which were published in 1978 as *An Autobiography of Values*.

> Science, freedom, beauty, adventure: what more could you ask of life? Aviation combined all the elements I loved. There was science in each curve of an airfoil, in each angle between strut and wire, in the gap of a spark plug or the color of the exhaust flame. There was freedom in the unlimited horizon, on the open fields where one landed. A pilot was surrounded by beauty of earth and sky. He brushed treetops with the birds, leapt valleys and rivers, explored the cloud canyons he had gazed at as a child. Adventure lay in each puff of wind.
>
> I began to feel that I lived on a higher plane than the skeptics on the ground – one that was richer because of its very association with the element of danger they dreaded, because it was freeer of the earth to which they were bound. In flying, I tasted a wine of the gods of which they could know nothing. Who valued life

Charles Lindbergh and the Spirit of St Louis

© Bettmann / Corbis

more highly, the aviators who spent it on the art they loved, or those misers who doled it out like pennies through their ant-like days? I decided that if I could fly for ten years before I was killed in a crash, it would be a worthwhile trade for an ordinary lifetime.

Charles A Lindbergh
1902-1974

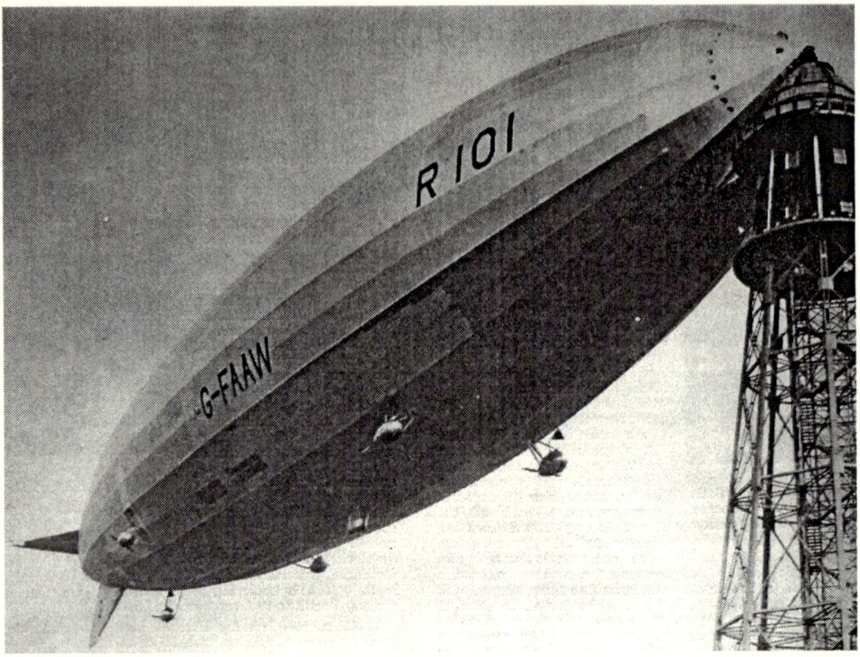

Saturday, October 4th, 1930
(Flight)

Sunday, October 5th, 1930
(Flight)

To England
Lord Darling, 1930

One of the most shocking events in the history of British aviation was the loss of HM Airship R101 on Sunday, 5th October, 1930. On her inaugural flight to India with many of the aviation dignitaries of the day on board, the airship crashed in northern France and, because hydrogen was the gas that was then used to support the airship, was completely destroyed by fire, killing 48 out of 54 people on board. This event led directly to the demise of the airship and, despite a few current versions filled with the inert gas helium, its popularity as a means of transport never recovered.

Charles Darling, then Lord Chief Justice of England, wrote this moving poem which was published first in *The Times*, and then in the 10th October, 1930 issue of *Flight*.

Mourn! Not despairing, as should hope depart –
When great thy grief, be thou thyself more great;
For ease thou wast not made: lift up thy heart
By trial formed to triumph over fate.

See, through thy tears, heroic faces beam
Of those thy sons who for the love of thee
Assailed the skies, to fall in faith supreme
That thou the conquest they have missed shall see.

Be brave to bear, as they were bold to soar;
Abandon not the aery paths they trod;
And, for their sake, endeavour thou the more
To take the way that bore their souls to God.

Lord Darling
1849-1936

Amelia Earhart, 1897-1937
(Flight)

Courage is the Price
Amelia Earhart

There can be few people with any interest in aviation who have not heard of the famous American aviatrix, Amelia Earhart. Born in 1897 she learned to fly in 1921 and in 1928 was the first woman to cross the Atlantic by air, albeit as a passenger. Subsequently she became the first woman to fly the Atlantic solo for which feat Congress awarded her the Distinguished Flying Cross. There followed a further five years of record breaking flying and fame before she took off with Fred Noonan in a Lockheed Electra twin to make a world flight in 1937; they disappeared over the Pacific and were never found.

Courage is the price that
Life exacts for granting peace.

The soul that knows it not
Knows no release from little things:
Knows not the livid loneliness of fear,
Nor mountain heights where bitter joy can hear the sound of wings.

Nor can life grant us boon of living, compensate
For dull gray ugliness and pregnant hate
Unless we dare
The soul's dominion.
Each time we make a choice, we pay
With courage to behold the restless day,
And count it fair.

Amelia Earhart
1897-1937

Dominion Over Air
C.A.F.B.

I have been unable to discover the identity of CAFB who wrote this poem. As it first appeared in the RAF Cranwell College journal and then in *Icarus: An anthology of the Poetry of Flight* it must have been written before 1939. The third line was one that inspired the young Magee when he wrote *High Flight*.

The winds of heaven urge, in freedom, vast
Ephemeral structure of the cloud domain
Across the unpierced sanctity of space,
Where yearns the virgin ether, still and vain.
There arc by arc, the sun unerringly
Moves on to squander, day by swift-drawn day,
All sum of time, while the moon and myriad stars
Preside in multitude of pale array.
Here now the vanquisher puts forth his wing
From earth, of earth, the blazing sky to rend,
A moving shadow on the firmament –
Another, and a conquered, world to spend.

C.A.F.B.

London to Paris by Air
Lord Gorell

This wonderfully descriptive poem by Lord Gorell (see *In The Air,* p.53) – "the kingdom of the breeze parts not the nations like the severing seas" – must have been the result of one of the many flights he had to make during his spell in office as Under-Secretary of State for Air from 1921 to 1922.

I

The droning roar is quickened, and we lift
On steady wing like upward sweep of air,
Into the fleece-strewn heaven. The great plane
Draws to herself the leagues: onward we bear
In one resistless eddy towards the south
Over the English fields, trim-hedged and square,
And countless winding lanes, a vast expanse
Of flattened green: huge shapes of shadow float
Inconsequent as bubbles: haunts of men
Stripped of their cherished privacy we note
And crawling multitudes within a town –
On all we rangers of the wind look down.

II

The coast-line swings to us: beneath our feet
The grey-green carpet of the sliding sea
Stretches afar, on it small, busy ships
Whose comet tails in foamy whiteness flee:
We lift, and snowy cloudlets roam below,
Frail, wistful spirits of pure charity
Blessing the waters: like green marble veined,
The waves roll in upon the yellowing sand,
Then break to myriad , filmy curves of lace
Where they eternally caress the land:

JANUARY 29, 1920 FLIGHT

(From an original drawing by Roderic Hill

"THE PARIS Mail": A D.H. 16 and a Handley Page passing each other over the English coast

Now low lies France – the kingdom of the breeze
Parts not the nations like the severing seas.

III

Down the wide river, jauntily outspread,
A fishing fleet comes seaward, to our eyes
Mere walnut shells with autumn leaves for sails:
And now a fellow pilgrim of the skies,
Like a big insect droning past our flank,
Cruises to England home: before us lies
The rolling plain with its great, hedgeless strips
Of close-tilled fields, red roofs, and pointed trees,
The feathered arrows of the long French roads,
And all the stretch of quiet harmonies:
Then haven shows, and downward to earth's breast,
Like homing bird, we wheel and sink to rest.

Ronald Barnes, 3rd Baron Gorell
1884-1963

New World
G W M Dunn

This poem is one of those in *Icarus: An Anthology of the Poetry of Flight* which influenced the young Magee when he wrote *High Flight*. Both 'laughter silvered wings' and 'lifting mind', two powerfully descriptive but hitherto unique phrases, feature in Dunn's great poem on the discovery and the promise of aviation.

Once again, sadly, I have been unable to trace any further record of the poet other than that a collection of his poetry was published in 1934 by Cape, entitled *Poems – Group One*.

This is the new world where my great wings take me
With powered laughter and shouting of the air
Far from the sounds of earth and straight-ruled ways
Where men's desires and feuds are drowned, to where
Solitude is great music and the days
Stretch over the roof of the world to welcome me.

Never the aching murmur of sad strings,
Drum-tap of grief or plaintive dirge of reeds;
With zest we soar on laughter-silvered wings
From fevered ways, panic and petty deeds,
Glad to upbear our cargo of earth's best,
For thought's high distillation, and man's rest.

We have killed lust and fear and jealousy,
The body's turmoil and the coward hand.
We are made whole from withering care
To surge the vast heart's song up from the land.
Rise to rejoice upon the spacious air
From the earth's fetters and the shackling sea.

The clouds and sky have neither words nor flowers;
There's no bewilderment of brain or sense,
Only the hushed limbs and lifting mind
Striving to heights beyond the hills and dense
Dark custom-mist which stills the spirit's wind;
From season's change and darkening of the hours.

Here no man touches me or flung stone wounds,
The store of earth is gathered for our strength
To temper to a high tenacity,
Raising man's wisdom to an unknown length,
Purging the faithless heart's inconstancy;
For love of man we fly on lonely winds.

No word is wasted: body, soul and mind
Lift ordered music out of the ken of man
In climb to freedom. Here's no hand to guide,
No staff for brief support, no praise, no ban.
We only know the perilous ways we ride
Through the charged silence of the earth-wise wind.

This is the new world, purged of woe and heart-break,
Where the great clouds are set in rank, and range
Stilled to the bidding word, the chastening hand,
Divorced from petty custom, here the strange
Huge spaces of the mind are all our land.
Soar to our heights, winged nations, for man's sake.

GWM Dunn

Kenneth Gandar Dower, 1908-1944

Amateur Adventure
Kenneth Gandar-Dower

Although he died at the early age of thirty-eight, Kenneth Cecil Gandar-Dower packed his life with sport and adventure. A consummate ball-games player he learnt to fly in 1932 and, with a friend, immediately piloted a DH Puss Moth from England to India. Explorations in Kenya and the Belgian Congo followed and in 1937 he introduced cheetah racing to England, disproving that the greyhound was the fastest animal in the world. A war correspondent during the Second World War, he was a passenger on the *SS Khedive Ismail* when, on a voyage from Mombasa to Colombo, she was torpedoed and sunk by a Japanese submarine on 12th February, 1944. His was one of the 1,297 lives lost.

This short poem, which was a preface to *Amateur Adventure*, his book about the flight to India, captures beautifully the excitement of the start of a great aerial journey.

Then roaring down the corridors of space
I will be still, and watch the world go by,
Till dull, known fields and cities of my race
Merge to grey dimness in a grim grey sky.

East to the dawn and southward to the sun
Borne on aloft by man's great gift of wings
To legend lands that make the pulses run
And towns that leap with names of ancient kings.

Kenneth Gandar-Dower
1908-1944

When I Was Twenty-One
Kenneth Gandar-Dower

His Harrow Housemaster wrote the Introduction to Gandar Dower's *Abyssinian Patchwork*. In it he described him as 'competitive, yet generous, loving yet agnostic, ambitious yet altruistic, the most loyal of friends and a pacifist determined to survive the war. Yet he wouldn't have safety on any terms, forever running headlong towards danger". When he was twenty-one, Gandar Dower wrote this poem about the prospect of crashing into the sea.

That will be the life. To feel the engines' power,
Their brave, strong purr, to reach at last the crest
Of my lone island in the sunset hour,
And dipping down the dusk to come to rest.

That will be life. Perchance some day the purr
Will die. Perchance at nightfall I shall find
On the great ocean disc no deeper blur –
That will be death, striking remote and blind.

When, in that hurried moment, out of sight
Of friends, when waves rush up to meet the air,
I find I do not wake, a child at night –
That will be death. I do not care.

I shall not see the glory fade,
The vision pass away,
Or mind and muscle shrink dismayed
Beneath a slow decay.
Ere cracked and tuneless rings the bell,
Ere clouds obscure the sun,
Ere broken be the golden spell

And summer days be done,
At least I shall have died right well
When I was twenty-one.

Kenneth Gandar Dower
1908-1944

The Seaplane
Louise Stewart

De la Bere and his assistants found this poem for inclusion in *Icarus*, published in 1939, and they acknowledged the author but made no mention of a previous publisher or where Louise's work had been printed. I have failed to find any trace of her – which is sad.

Each night across the sunset skies
I watch a sailorman who flies.
Swifter than swallows are his wings
Mounting to where the pale moon swings
Above the solan's* forked flight.
Far, far above the mad waves' spite
I catch his throbbing, laughing song,
Exultant 'neath the stars' bright throng,
While chasing cloud flotillas he
Conquers the air as well as sea.

* gannet

Louise Stewart

The Night Mail
Naomi C Katz

Throughout the 1920s and '30s much of the development of civil aviation was centred around the carriage of mail, as delivery by air was so much faster than the previous surface methods of road, rail and ship. But once promised, and to warrant its cost, the delivery of air mail had to be reliable whatever the many reasons for non-delivery. Many pilots' lives were lost trying to deliver the mail, mainly because of adverse weather conditions.

The last line of Naomi Katz's poem is timeless.

The black rain falls down in steady pour;
The stormy heavens flash a blinding light,
Now bar the windows up, and shut the door;
Not even a bird would brave the world tonight.

Not even a bird? – Above the thunder's drum
I hear the sound of someone there who flies,
Someone who travels with a roaring hum-m-m,
In a high ship with yellow lights for eyes.

The wet wind sweeps him from his path;
Around him white hot bolts of lightning play;
The thunder hurls at him its booming wrath –
And he goes calmly on his zig-zag way.

What is the cargo that he carried there?
How is it precious, that it cannot wait?
Oh! You who tempt the heavens, have a care!
But he goes forward like unchanging Fate.

Forward and upward! with a steady sail;
Battling his way across the furious skies –
Night after night he carries on the mail;
And none will know his name, unless he dies.

Naomi C. Katz
1896-1969

Flight
Ethel De B Lasky

I can find nothing about the author to date this poem accurately but it appeared in *Wings: An Anthology of Flight*, published in 1942. It is a fine tribute to those men and women who continued to expand the realms of aviation during the Golden Age, the final verse constituting a fitting inscription on any memorial to aviation pioneers.

Climbing the levels of air they come,
 Swift as never an eagle flew,
Pioneers of the rolling cloud –
 The reaching wind – the abysmal blue.

Mountain and desert echo the drone
 Of the great grey birds that sing as they go;
Rivers mirror the tireless wings;
 Oceans throb and thunder below.

Does the news flash out to a host unseen –
 Columbus, Peary, all souls of fire
Whose courage ventured the unattained
 And won to the peak of a high desire?

Does the heart of Magellan quicken and beat,
 As it slumbers far from the coast of Spain,
Dream of a dim horizon line
 And the gleam of a virgin wave again?

Sky and sea shall remember them,
 And men in honour their names shall write
Who have woven around the spinning world
 The magic golden girdle of flight.

Ethel De B Lasky

Prize WInners, RAF College, Cranwell, 1938
F./C. U./O. Brian Pashley Young with sword of honour
(Photo: Gale & Polden, Aldershot. By kind permission of RAF College, Cranwell)

Flight
Brian Young

This is another poem worthy of its place in Adrian Swire's flying log-book. The author is Air Vice Marshal Brian Pashley Young who had a distinguished wartime and peacetime career in the RAF and RAF Regiments. A South African, he was a cadet at RAF Cranwell in 1936; was awarded the Sword of Honour and was commissioned in 1938. The following year his poem appeared in *Icarus – an Anthology of the Poetry of Flight*, so was written before he was 21. In celebration of his winning the Sword of Honour?

How can they know that joy to be alive
 Who have not flown?
To loop and spin and roll and climb and dive,
 The very sky one's own,
The urge of power while engines race,
 The sting of speed,
The rude winds' buffet on one's face,
 To live indeed.

How can they know the grandeur of the sky,
 The earth below,
The restless sea, and waves that break and die
 With ceaseless ebb and flow;
The morning sun on drifting clouds
 And rolling downs –
And valley mist that shrouds
 The chimneyed towns?

So long has puny man to earth been chained
  Who now is free,
And with the conquest of the air has gained
  A glorious liberty.
How splendid is this gift He gave
  On high to roam,
The sun a friend, the earth a slave,
  The heavens home.

Air Vice-Marshal Brian Pashley Young, CB, CBE, RAF
1918-1992

The Second World War 1939-1945

Introduction

The Golden Age saw the transition of the biplane to the monoplane, the fixed pitch to the variable pitch propeller, the fixed to the retractable undercarriage, the open to the closed cockpit. It saw the introduction of inverted engines with superchargers – horse-powers going up tenfold; speeds to several hundreds of miles per hour and ranges from hundreds to thousands of miles; aircraft could lift tons instead of pounds of cargo. The world powers equipped their air forces with aircraft incorporating all these developments and woe betide any country that lagged behind. With European, if not World, domination in mind Germany tested her air force in the Spanish Civil War so that when the Second World War was declared in 1939, she had battle-proven aircrews and aircraft ready for action.

With the development of the aeroplane warfare in the air took on a far greater importance than in the previous conflict and the numbers of aircrew and casualties far exceeded those of the First World War.

The earlier conflict was largely restricted to Europe whereas the second Armageddon truly encompassed the whole world, facilitated by the enormous range of the combatants' air forces and the advent of the aircraft carrier.

The early war poetry still reflected the wonderment of young men taking to the air for the first time but quickly turned to the realities of modern aerial warfare resulting in disillusion and dismay at the awful casualties, particularly the disfigurement that fire in the air wreaked on aircrews whose aircraft were able to carry them home despite enormous damage. The sound of the 'thousand bomber' raids flown by boys still in their teens reminded the civilian population nightly of the awful destruction being meted out by the vengeful allies.

Women played a far greater role in this war and their devoted attendance on the wounded and the dying resulted in their writing some of the most moving poetry of those years.

Individual aerial combat by the fighter pilots, particularly during the Battle of Britain, created new heroes, leaving the far greater but less romantic casualties suffered by the bomber crews to much delayed recognition although poets like Noel Coward and Sarah Churchill captured the relentlessness of aerial bombardment which ultimately brought the Axis to their knees.

"These who were children yesterday..."
Hurricane pilots somewhere in England, 1940
(Flight)

Youth in the Skies
Herbert Asquith

Herbert Asquith was the second son of Herbert Henry Asquith, the Liberal Prime Minister from 1908 to 1916. His poetry was greatly affected by his service in the Royal Artillery during the First World War.

These who were children yesterday
Now move in lovely flight,
Swift-glancing as the shooting stars
That cleave the summer night;

A moment flashed, they came and went,
Horizons rise and fall,
The speed of valour lifts them up
And strength obeys their call.

The downs below are breathing peace
With thyme and butterflies,
And sheep at pasture in the shade –
And now from English skies.

These who were children yesterday
Look down with other eyes:
Man's desperate folly was not theirs
But theirs the sacrifice.

Old men may wage a war of words,
Another race are these,
Who flash to glory dawn and night
Above the starry seas.

Herbert Asquith
1881-1947

Timothy John Manley Corsellis, 1921-1941

The R.A.F.
Timothy Corsellis, 11th September 1940

Having read Patricia Ledward's requiem poem for Timothy Corsellis (page 328), but not having found any of his own work, I was delighted to discover that his younger brother John, now aged 89, had invited Helen Goethals, Professor of Commonwealth Literature at Toulouse University, to write a book, to be published shortly, of Timothy's verse and life under the title *The Unassuming Sky*. This account gives long overdue credit to Timothy's poems, one hundred of which are in the book, most for the first time, only a few examples of his poetry having been published during the war in Britain and America.

Timothy Corsellis was a devout Christian while at Winchester and a pacifist when he left the school. He joined the Royal Air Force during the Battle of Britain but while under training was streamed to bombers, whereupon he resigned on the principle that he had joined the RAF to defend his country and not to bomb civilians. He was, astonishingly, given an honourable discharge whereupon he joined the Air Transport Auxiliary (ATA), that wonderful band of men and women pilots formed by Sir Gerard d'Erlanger at the beginning of the Second World War. Their job was to fly the thousands of aircraft produced by Britain's aircraft industry from the factories to the operational airfields, thereby leaving the pilots of the Royal Air Force to concentrate on operational flying. Their record of safe delivery of those aircraft was magnificent.

I threw my whole self into the strife
And swept aside restrictive tape
I know that I have stepped from life
Into a whirlwind of escape.

I offered my body up to pain
My mind I gave as an army's toy
To organised evil I turned my brain,
But all I feel is joy.

I thrill to the shuddering laugh of a gun
Furious and free in the open air
I glory in every deed that I've done
In all my short search for fear.

Timothy Corsellis
1921-1941

What I Never Saw
Timothy Corsellis, 24th January 1941

This was to be the last and best-liked poem that Timothy Corsellis wrote while he was still in the RAF. When doing his elementary flying training he had met and liked the colonial pilots who he described as "a much nicer lot than the Englishers, mostly from Kenya".

I was ready for death
Ready to give my all in an expansive gesture
For a cause that was worthy of death.
I wanted to fear, to watch blood and torture
To draw my last breath
Amidst a chaos of dramatic thunder
I dreamt of the aeroplanes sweeping the sky
Gave war her ghastly lure
Came ready to fight and to die.

I thought in my mufti
Of brave men marching to battle
And came here to join them
To share the machine guns rattle
But I never expected
The weary hours of waiting while the sun rose and set
The everlasting eye turned upwards to the sky
Watching the weather which said
Thou shalt not fly.

We sat together as we sat at peace
Bound by no ideal of service
But by a common interest in pornography
And a pride to outdrink one another.
War was remote
There was a little trouble in Abyssinia
Some of us came from Kenya and said,
"Why I was on the spot all the while and the
Italians sprayed the roadside with mustard gas."

They could all tell stories of war.

Then came the queuing
The recurrent line of pungent men
Dressed in dirt with mud eating at their trouser legs
The collar that is cleaner than the shirt
And the inevitable adjectives.

The papers ran out early today
There was no butter for the bread at breakfast
Nobody calls us at dawn
We never strain or sweat
Nor do they notice when we come in late.

When I was a civilian I hoped high
Dreamt my future cartwheels in the sky
Almost forgot to arm myself
Against the boredom and the inefficiency
The petty injustice and the everlasting grudges
The sacrifice is greater than I ever expected.

Timothy Corsellis
1921-1941

Coldly Land Slipped Away
Timothy Corsellis, 2nd September 1941

In February 1941, Timothy Corsellis had completed his elementary flying training with the RAF. Following his honourable discharge (he had unsuccessfully applied for a transfer to the Fleet Air Arm) it took him until August before he was able to join the Air Transport Auxiliary (ATA). This poem celebrated his return to flying as an ATA pilot.

Coldly land slipped away below our feet
Placid and dormant after we had spurned
Its incident-impelled existence. And the beat
Of the open air thrilled upwards to our brains.

We felt that while we stood upon the field
Earth with her tentacles of fear held us in chains
Now that we know not what the skies may yield
Fear becomes laughter, space our prison cell.

Bravely upon the earth we worked our way
Through the eternal striving to our needs
Flew and discovered in the sky our place of play
Where fear and future have no power to harm.

Placid below us lay the unfaltering earth
Yet unaware that we escape her realm
Our laughter in the skies won us a second birth
A life among the clouds alone in space.

At school they taught us that we moved in three
Dimensions, bounding in the human world
Little they saw the coming day when we
Would spurn all boundaries in space's gaseous sea.

You who remain imprisoned in these walls
Know nothing of that movement in the sky
And will be unprepared when the Creator calls
And gives to you the freedom that we know, who fly.

Timothy Corsellis
1921-1941

A Young English Airman
John Masefield, 1940

After an unhappy education at King's School, Warwick, John Masefield went to HMS Conway "to train for a life at sea, and to break his addiction to reading". But after a few years at sea he deserted ship to become a writer. In 1930, after a prodigious output of poetry, and over the favourite for the post, Rudyard Kipling, Masefield was appointed Poet Laureate and held this title until his death in 1967. Throughout his life he encouraged the continued development of English literature and instituted the award of Royal Medals for Poetry.

At the age of 24 his first collected works were published including one of his most famous poems *Sea Fever*. Many people, including the author, have written an aviation parody of this poem; in my case it was because I thought that Masefield had not written an aviation poem. I was wrong and I have selected this sonnet and two more of his aviation poems for this anthology.

This fine tribute to a young English pilot who was killed in the Battle of France first appeared in *The Nine Days Wonder*, Masefield's account of the evacuation of 338,000 British and French soldiers from the beaches at Dunkirk. Barely one month later these events were overtaken by the equally desperate circumstances of the Battle of Britain.

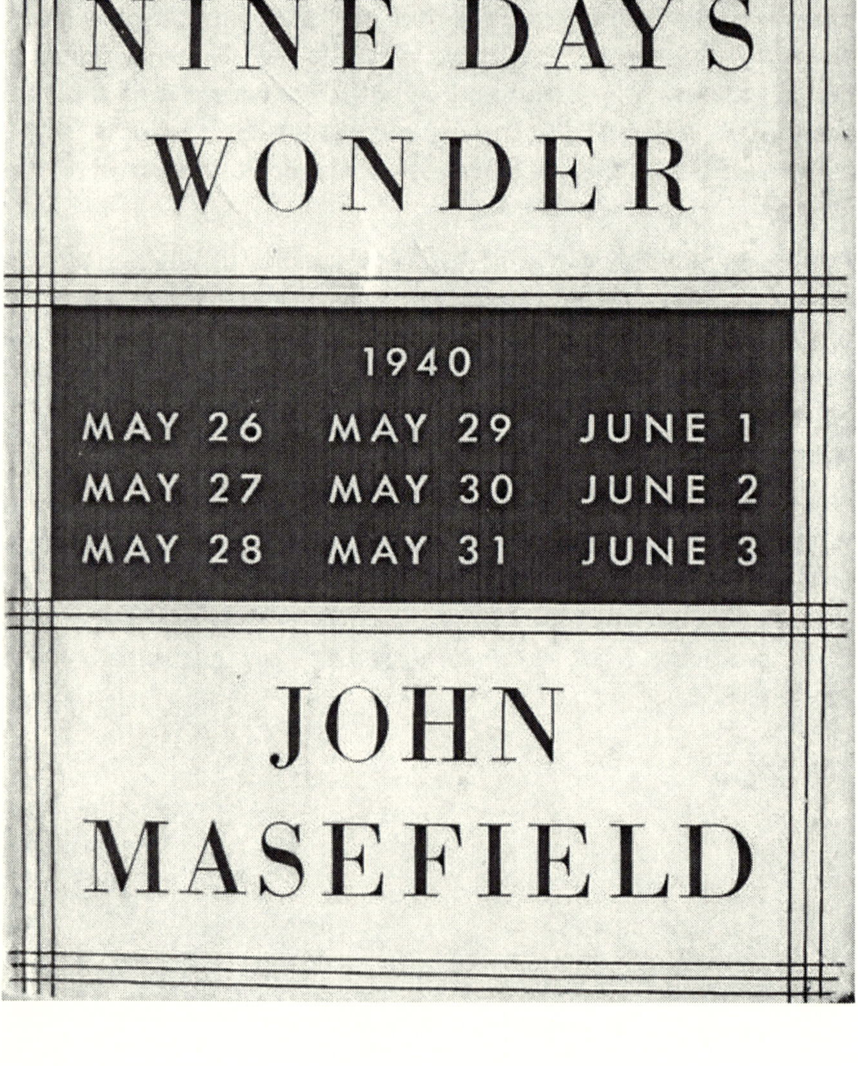
THE
NINE DAYS
WONDER
1940
MAY 26 MAY 29 JUNE 1
MAY 27 MAY 30 JUNE 2
MAY 28 MAY 31 JUNE 3
JOHN
MASEFIELD

O smiling sun-burned youth who rode the sky
Like to the sparrow-hawk or summer swift,
And watched your shadow flitting on the drift
Far underneath you as you hurried by,

Six months ago today you put off bird
To gleam as iron in a nation's will,
To save the ruined friends and then lie still,
Spring never to be touched by summer's word.

Often unseen by those you helped to save
You rode the air above that foreign dune
And died like the unutterably brave
That so your friends might see the English June.

Haply, in some sharp instant in mid-sky,
When you, at bird's summit, took the lunge
Of the foe's bitterness that made you die,
And the bright bird declined into her plunge,

You, from the Heaven, saw, in English chalk
White, about Dover, some familiar track,
That feet of yours would never again walk
Since you were killed and never coming back,

Yet knew, that your young life, as price paid over
Let thousands live to tread that track to Dover.

John Masefield, OM, Poet Laureate
1878-1967

Fighter Boy
A lone Hurricane pilot dons his flying kit, 1940
(Flight)

Fighter Boy
Nigel Norman

At the outbreak of the Second World War, Nigel Norman, now in the Royal Auxiliary Air Force, was posted to France and wrote this poem in November, 1939, after a visit to 11 Group's Emergency Refuelling Unit in the Lille Section. We can safely assume that he encountered pilots of the Royal Air Force flying Hurricanes in support of the British Expeditionary Force prior to its evacuation from the beaches at Dunkirk between 26th May and 3rd June, 1940.

At the end of the book of Nigel's collected poems, called simply *Verses 1911 – 1943*, his eldest son, Mark Norman, recounted his father's tragic death in 1943, two days before his forty-sixth birthday.

"Although due to become Lord Tedder's Chief Operations Officer, he was on that day taking the 'shuttle', a Lockheed Hudson, from Cornwall to Tunis. He and his opposite number, General 'Boy' Browning, had arrived to see Churchill in General Eisenhower's B17 and were due to return a few days later. Nigel decided to go back earlier to sort out changes, just agreed, to the plans for the airborne invasion of Sicily. The Hudson's port engine failed soon after take-off. Nigel, standing behind the two pilots, was just able to enter the cabin and shout to those inside to take up crash positions before the aircraft hit the ground. He did not have time to do so and was killed instantly. All but the radio operator, who died later, were saved by his prompt warning. Nigel Norman's flying log-books were with him when his aircraft burned. Fortunately his poems were not."

Drink – but with an unsoured stomach;
  Girls – but with a young man's touch;
Cards, but with no care for money,
  Scarred by life – but not too much.

See him go, with footsteps scraping;
  Soaking flying boots worn down,
Oil-stained, tattered, coat misshaping
  Athlete's figure into clown;

Hair untidy – tie a bootlace,
  What a marvellous disguise,
If you couldn't guess his true place,
  If you couldn't read his eyes!

Smooth that hand on stick and trigger,
  Tiger-like in air that tread!
Gun-kid with a thousand horses,
  And a price upon his head!

Air Commodore Sir Nigel Norman RAF
1897-1943

RAF, May, 1940
Sylvia Lynd

This poem, written by Sylvia Lynd, poet and novelist, appears in *Shadows of War*, edited by Anne Powell, a wonderful collection of poetry written by women during the Second World War. Sylvia Lynd makes the novel suggestion that Bomber Command should be forever commemorated by re-naming some of the great constellations in its honour.

Heard the squadron flying home
At midnight high among the stars;
Never did tale of Greece or Rome
Tell of such heroes or such wars.

Legend nor boast nor history
Proclaim such deeds as these achieve,
Who daily fight Thermopylae,
Who snatch the glove from Death, and live.

Perseus and Bellerophon,
They, too, were fighters and had wings,
They fought with monsters and they won,
And in the stars their glory rings.

Castor and Pollux keep their station,
Neither do we dispute their claim
If a more glorious constellation
Should mark a still more glorious fame.

Instead of Bear, or Wain, or Plough,
Splendid to see in night's great dome,
Give to those stars a new name now,
Call them the Squadron Flying Home.

Sylvia Lynd
1888-1952

John Pudney, 1909-1977
© Bryan Wharton, Collection National Portrait Gallery, London, x88644

For Johnny
John Pudney

Having worked as a radio producer, script writer and war correspondent, John Pudney joined the Royal Air Force in 1940, ending as a Squadron Leader and serving in Africa, the Mediterranean and France.

This was probably his most famous poem. Written on the back of an envelope during an air-raid on London in 1941, it captured the mood of the war in the air at the time.

Do not despair
For Johnny-head-in-air;
He sleeps as sound
As Johnny underground.

Fetch out no shroud
For Johnny-in-the-cloud;
And keep your tears
For him in after years.

Better by far
For Johnny-the-bright-star,
To keep your head,
And see his children fed.

John Pudney
1909-1977

Sonnet to a Windsock
W D O'Hanlon, December 1940

At the end of 1940 the Works Department replaced the windsock at the north end of Biggin Hill airfield, not fifty yards from the bomb shelter where forty WAAFs were killed in one of the many raids this key fighter base suffered.

Can there be a more powerful description in only one and a half lines, of Spitfires and Hurricanes taking off during the Battle of Britain, than 'Towards you my visored friends, with one last glance, unleashed their Merlins...'?

W D O'Hanlon was the Chaplain at RAF Biggin Hill from 1940 to 1942.

Bravo canvas on a thousand breezes borne,
Now on some scrapheap destined to be thrown,
By bullets riddled, and bomb splinters torn,
These fateful months you faithfully have flown.
For bloodshot eyes within the circuit flying,
The wind's own eye precisely you have found; –
Young men – and some are hurt and some are dying, –
At ninety knots they glide from air to ground.
Towards you my visored friends, with one last glance,
Unleashed their Merlins – took off into cloud,
James fell in flames and Christopher in France,
For Peter and for Simon sea was shroud.
Shall 'danger-money' workmen end your year?
'Give it me please'! Young voices fill my ear.

W D O'Hanlon

Battle of Britain Pilot
Audrey Grealy

Audrey Grealy was born in 1922 and has had a life-long interest in flying and the Royal Air Force. She met her future husband in 1952, only later discovering that in 1943 he had become, at the age of 19, a bomb-aimer, serving a tour of operations on Lancaster bombers with 12 Squadron. Later he became a navigator only retiring from the RAF in 1972. Audrey has been writing poetry since childhood and published her own book of poetry about the RAF in both world wars called *The Sky Their Battlefield*, now sadly out of print.

He had not long left sixth form days behind
A gangling boy with unassuming smile
His youth dissolved within the tidal surge
Of urgent training, practice, speed and guile
Of learning, in a travesty of time
The tricks of eagle, hawk and rising lark
His eyes and brain and limbs a molten whole
Fused by a vital all-consuming spark.
The hot September sun burned fierce and clear
The vapour trails etched patterns in the sky
A brilliant blue celestial battlefield
In which to fly, to fight, to kill, to die.
He lived a strange encapsulated life
Of scrambles, engines, oil and glycol smells
Sleep to be taken when and as he could
In rare and precious interrupted spells.
His world of bandits, angels, spins and kites
Was only known to those who shared his way
Of living each free moment as it came
To drain the essence of each passing day
To revel in the love of pretty girls

To drive a car as though it were a plane
To laugh like schoolboys playing daring pranks
To test the potency of hop and grain
To keep his mind detached and sharp and cool
When old new friends went spiralling down in flames
To thrust aside the sudden pain of loss
And give no quarter to the icy claims
That fear might make in one unguarded thought
Of being blinded, paralysed or trapped
To roast inside a blazing cockpit hood
In burning clothing swaddled and enwrapped.
He fought his war above the patchwork fields
And golden fruited orchards far below
He played the noisy party games and sang
The bawdy songs that only airmen know.
He lived a lifetime's share of vibrant joy
And spurned the dull materialistic things
He lasted seven weeks, his destined span
And death received him gently in her wings.

Audrey Grealy
1922-

Air Chief Marshal Sir Christopher Foxley-Norris introducing HM Queen Elizabeth the Queen Mother to a Battle of Britain veteran at the unveiling of the memorial on 9th July, 1993

Envoi – Battle of Britain Pilot
Christopher Foxley-Norris

Christopher Foxley-Norris was a Battle of Britain pilot, flying Hurricanes with 3 Squadron during the last few weeks of the battle. He went on to a distinguished life-time career in the Royal Air Force, eventually retiring in 1954.

His obituary in *The Independent* described him as "one of the best-known personalities of the Royal Air Force... a fine leader who recognised the importance of acknowledging the contribution of his subordinates and trusting them to do their jobs properly... he possessed too that all-important quality, a sense of humour, although his reluctance to take himself or others too seriously sometimes ruffled feathers in high places".

He will always be remembered as an untiring Chairman of the Battle of Britain Association by the Foxley-Norris Wall at the Battle of Britain Memorial at Chapel le Ferne, Dover which lists the names of every allied pilot – the immortal Few – who flew in that battle.

Remember him?
He was no Galahad, no knight sans peur et sans reproche.
Sans peur? Fear was the second enemy to beat. He was
a common, unconsidered man who, for a brief moment of
eternity,
Held the whole future of mankind in his two sweating
palms
And did not let it go.
Remember him,
Not as he was portrayed but as he was. To him
You owe the most of what you have and love today.

Air Chief Marshal Sir Christopher Foxley-Norris, GCB, DSO, OBE
1917-2003

The Price – 1940
Audrey Grealy

It is still not generally known how much was owed to the Polish pilots who fought in the Battle of Britain. After the fall of Poland at the beginning of the Second World War many Poles made their way to Britain to continue the fight against Nazi Germany, among them battle-hardened pilots who had been in action against the Luftwaffe. They eventually made up several Hurricane and Spitfire squadrons of whom Air Chief Marshal Sir Hugh Dowding, C-in-C Fighter Command during the battle, commented that without their contribution the result might have been very different.

English pilot, young and eager,
Still not even twenty-one,
Giving in the cloudless skies
The life that had but scarce begun,
Falling like a blazing comet...
Someone's brother, someone's son.

German pilot, keen and youthful,
Many years of life to spend,
Shot down over English meadows,
Fighting to the bitter end,
Burning in the flaming aircraft...
Someone's husband, someone's friend.

Polish pilot, battle-hardened,
Sad at heart with worldly strife,
Ties of family and homeland
Cut as by a searing knife,
Dying in his bloodstained cockpit…
Someone's lover, someone's life.

Audrey Grealy
1922-

A Layman's Glimpse (an extract)
Lord David Cecil, 1942

Lord Edward Christian David Gascoigne Cecil was the youngest son of the 4th Marquess of Salisbury. After Eton and Christ Church, Oxford he became a Fellow of Wadham College, Oxford, where he taught history and literature. He then became Professor of English Literature at New College, Oxford, a post he held from 1948 to 1969. His specialty was writing biographies and he accompanied Sir William Rothenstein when he was commissioned by the Air Ministry to write about, and sketch, the men of the RAF. Rothenstein made 147 sketches of officers and men of the junior service and the result of their visits was *Men of the RAF*, published in 1942, which included 40 of Rothenstein's brilliant crayon sketches. Cecil wrote for it a piece called *A Layman's Glimpse*. It is one piece of writing that I particularly wanted to enclose in my anthology; first, because I do not think many people know of it and secondly, because it captures perfectly the essential character of those men of the Royal Air Force who did so much to help win the Second World War. I hope that today's young men and women might emulate them.

> Indeed the spectacle of the RAF is an antidote to melancholy in more ways than one. Some people nowadays take a gloomy view of the future. They think the world is changing; and they fear that, in the process of change, the qualities they value in our civilisation will vanish. A visit to the Air Force will prove them wrong. It could not be more modern, with its mechanised weapons, its democratic indifference to formality and class-distinction. Yet in other ways, in its individualism, its free gallant adventure, air warfare seems a reversion to that of an earlier day. Even it

harks back to those legendary ages when the radiant gods fought in the clouds above Troy. And the men engaged in it are the Englishmen of history, faithful and phlegmatic, chivalrous and ironical, imbued with that peculiarly English fortitude which contrives, without fanaticism, to be indomitable. These men flourish amid hangars and hurricanes as naturally as in the timbered hulks of Trafalgar. Why should we fear for the nation that gave them birth?

Lord David Cecil
1902-1986

Squadron Leader JS Dewar, DSO, DFC
Crayon sketch by Sir William Rothenstein

Men of the RAF (an extract)
Sir William Rothenstein

In his Foreword to Men of the RAF Air Chief Marshal Sir Charles Portal comments that Sir William Rothenstein 'has observed carefully and recorded with great artistry the types of men that he saw'. Rothenstein himself wrote with great feeling about these young men, many of whom would not see the end of the war. This piece was his observation of the pilots of Fighter Command.

The smiling airman of the illustrated press, looking up into the sky, showing two rows of white teeth, like fashionable beauties, I have nowhere seen. Cheerful enough they are. But their outlook on life is of necessity different from that of young men in peacetime. Most of us, even those more advanced in years, look forward and plan for the future. For these airmen, only the present and the past have reality; they look away, I imagine, from what may come. As for thinking: 'infinite meditation upon a pint pot wouldn't give us a gill of beer'. So their pleasures and dissipations are simple – visits to neighbouring towns, the pubs and cinemas. So, too, they read detective stories and light novels, which make little claim on their mental powers. In the mess they play bridge, billiards and ping-pong; draughts too, and a few played chess. In the room I occupied were some cheap novels, a book or two connected with flying, photographs of parents, of a sweetheart, and a reminder of what must ever be deep down in their consciousness, an envelope containing a will. Yet it would scarcely strike anyone coming into the mess, seeing the cheerful young men standing about the fire with bright tankards of beer in their hands, talking or reading in easy chairs, that a few hours earlier they were at their dangerous work of reconnaissance over enemy country, or convoying ships at any moment open to attack.

I wondered often what goes on in the secret shrine of the airman's mind. Impenetrable, even to his companions. I think of Frances Cornford's lines:

> A young Apollo, golden-haired,
> Stands dreaming on the verge of strife,
> Magnificently unprepared
> For the long littleness of life.

Yet these young men were getting a schooling through action, which many of us who are withdrawn from the active side of life may miss.

Whatever rumblings of coming upheavals may be discerned, they are muffled for airmen's ears by the din of the dreadful artillery of war. Sufficient for the moment that they have their immediate, definite task to carry out. 'I tell them to go there, and they go,' as a Station Commander said to me. They are not sicklied over with doubt, and I find their company good. If we question, with our imperfect knowledge, the morality of this or that, we may fail to find a clear answer. But of one moral issue in 'this endless war 'twixt truth and truth' we have no doubt – a thing can be well or ill done, and something deep in our nature makes us respect him who does his work well, and withhold our respect from the idler and the bungler. So one cannot overpraise these men, who carry out what is asked of them with incredible courage and an admirable resourcefulness. Mr. Churchill has put our debt to them concisely: 'Never have so many owed so much to so few'. It was a privilege to make drawings of such men.

Sir William Rothenstein
1872-1945

Engine Failure
Timothy Corellis, 2nd October 1941

This is one of the poems that was published during the war, and again in America at the end of the war where Timothy Corsellis gained earlier recognition as a poet than in England.

On 10th October, 1941, not two months after he joined the ATA, and only eight days after he wrote this poem, Timothy ferried a Miles Magister from White Waltham to Carlisle. On arrival he was seen circling the house of friends but while doing so he unaccountably crashed and was killed. He was only 20 years old.

We are used to the murmur
The regular rumble of holocaust power,
The turning propellers defying the air:
We are used to the thunder
The purposeful pounding of steel against steel,
The purring of pistons and petrol explosions.
But not
To the cough
The cacophony of failure,
A hope to recover,
A failure, a failure
The regular rumble irrupted
An engine has cut on the take-off
Broke, broke in the rhythm,
The seconds stand still for a pause
Then hurry their number on faster than speed
As precipitate fear of the pilot is pitched
To action,
  action rehearsed in pretence
Springs to reality, full fraught with fear
"The ground is uneven and hedges are there

"We'll aim for the right of the woods
"We'll try for this clearance here
"I've taken the wheels up
"Thank God that the wheels are unlocked.
"She'll clumsily crash on her stomach
"Her broad metal belly of steel
"And slithering slide to a standstill
"Or crash to the fear of the fence.
"This may be the end and the end."
We leapt from our chairs
At the first broken cough
At the first loss of power
"It's a Spitfire!" the cry
We rushed from the room
Avid to witness the wound
Watch the fear fraught, the fatal
Fracture of normal procedure.
We know him, we know him
One of our number in danger;
It might have been I
Goddam it, I wish it were I
With the will to thrill at the fear
And the danger of death that is near.
I wish it were I.

I heard the false laugh as she landed in safety
American* accent was cynically lifted.
"What are we doing? Goddam him he made it.
"No sights of despair for today."

Timothy Corsellis
1921-1941

* American pilot flew with the ATA before the USA joined the war on 9th December, 1941

High Flight
John Gillespie Magee, 1941

This sonnet is probably the most famous and most favourite celebration of flying in aviation poetry. There can be few airmen who have not heard it or read it; indeed many will know it by heart. Read at many funerals and memorial services, extracts were quoted by President Ronald Reagan at the memorial service for the crew of astronauts who were killed in the tragic explosion of the space shuttle *Challenger*.

Born in Shanghai to an American missionary father and an English mother Magee was sent first to St Clare's preparatory school near Walmer in Kent and then to Rugby. There he won the poetry prize thirty years after that same prize had been won by Rupert Brooke, one of the great English poets of the First World War and a strong influence on Magee.

Following Rugby Magee continued a brilliant scholastic career at Avon School, near Hartford, Connecticut and was accepted for entry to Yale. But impatient to fly he joined the Royal Canadian Air Force and was awarded his 'wings' at Uplands, Ontario in 1941. Posted to Landow in Wales he converted to Spitfires and it was there that he wrote his most famous poem.

In September 1941 he was posted to the all-Canadian 412 Squadron at Wellingore and briefly saw action in November of that year. On 11th December, 1941, while descending through cloud in a Spitfire at the end of a routine patrol he collided with an Airspeed Oxford training aircraft from RAF Cranwell; both pilots were killed. Magee was 19 when he died.

Oh! I have slipped the surly bonds of Earth
And danced the skies on laughter-silvered wings;
Sunward I've climbed, and joined the tumbling mirth

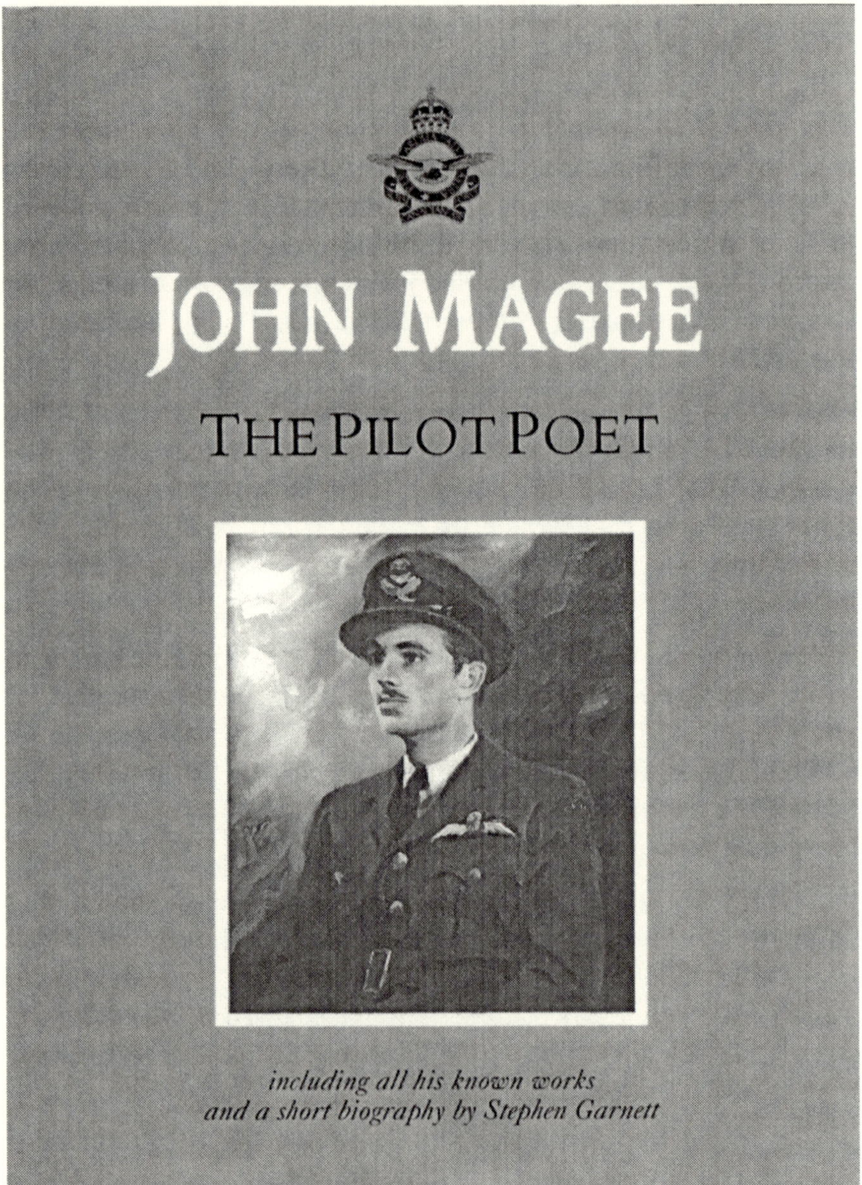
JOHN MAGEE
THE PILOT POET
including all his known works
and a short biography by Stephen Garnett

Of sun-split clouds – and done a hundred things
You have not dreamed of – wheeled and soared and swung
High in the sunlit silence. Hov'ring there,
I've chased the shouting wind along, and flung
My eager craft through footless halls of air.

Up, up the long delirious burning blue
I've topped the windswept heights with easy grace,
Where never lark nor even eagle flew –
And, while with silent, lifting mind I've trod
The high untrespassed sanctity of space,
Put out my hand and touched the face of God.

Pilot Officer John Gillespie Magee, RCAF
1922-1941

In recent years there has been some discussion as to the source of inspiration for Magee's poem.

Several phrases used by him appeared in other poems, all printed in 1938 in a book by R de la Bere, compiled with the help of four of his flight cadets at RAF Cranwell. The book was called *Icarus – an anthology of the poetry of flight*. With such an enquiring mind and passion for poetry it would be logical for Magee to have read this book avidly and to have tucked away such phrases as "laughter-silvered wings", "lifting mind", "shouting air" which appear in GWM Dunn's *New World*; "sanctity of space" from CAFB's *Dominion over Air*, and finally "danced the streets of heaven" and "touched the face of God" both of which appear in Cuthbert Hicks's remarkable *The Blind Man Flies*.

Is this plagiarism? There are only so many ways that a poet can describe the sensations of flight and for a young enthusiastic pilot poet to find these, remember them and weave them together into such a successful sonnet is in itself no small achievement. But for the young John to send the poem to his parents with the note that "It started at 30,000 feet and was finished soon after I landed" is surely poetic licence.

Oh Once Again
John Gillespie Magee, 1941

This is the final poem printed in the paperback version of *John Magee – The Pilot Poet*. The poem was missing from the first, hardback, edition which was printed in 1989 by This England Books; the paper-back was only printed in 1996, by which time Magee's family had found three more of his poems of which this was one.

To climb aloft and watch the dawn ascend
Earth's haze-enshrouded rim. To dally high
And see the morning ghosts forsake their blend
For sundry silhouettes. To catch the sky
Transformed, its fawn and silv'ry tints now rife
With brilliant hues recast. To ease my craft
Below as golden darts give birth to life
And set the world astir. To catch a shaft
Of beaming warmth, and quickened by its touch
Assault its course through hills of airy fleece.
To burst at last above the crests and clutch
The fleeting freedom – endless blue, at peace.

Pilot Officer John Gillespie Magee, RCAF
1922-1941

Per Ardua
John Gillespie Magee, 1941

This was the last poem written by Magee before his untimely death. Although it is not as well known as *High Flight* it nevertheless captures the feeling and spirit of the time. As a young pilot about to see active service after the Battle of Britain, he cannot have failed to have been inspired by 'The Few'. Sadly he was never to be able to show whether that great example would also help to make him a more effective fighter pilot.

Dedication: *To those who gave their lives to England during the Battle of Britain and left such a shining example to us who follow, these lines are dedicated.*

They that have climbed the white mists of the morning;
They that have soared, before the world's awake,
To herald up their foemen to them, scorning
The thin dawn's rest their weary folk might take;

Some that have left other mouths to tell the story
Of high, blue battle, – quite young limbs that bled;
How they had thundered up the clouds to glory
Or fallen to an English field stained red;

Because my faltering feet would fail I find them
Laughing beside me, steadying the hand
That seeks their deadly courage – yet behind them
The cold light dies in that once brilliant land...

Do these, who help the quickened pulse run slowly,
Whose stern remembered image cools the brow –
Till the far dawn of Victory know only
Night's darkness, and Valhalla's silence now?

Pilot Officer John Gillespie Magee, RCAF
1922-1941

Molly Corbally, 1913-2008

...Ad Astra
Molly Corbally, circa 1942

I found this touching poem by Molly Corbally, in *The Voice of War*. Molly was an SRN (State Registered Nurse) in the Territorial Army Nursing Service. She was called up in January 1940 and spent four years in the 19th General Field Hospital, Bitter Lakes, Egypt, tending the wounded of both sides and working with the eminent surgeon, Lieutenant-Colonel Professor Ian Aird. A compassionate woman, in post-war years she became a noted Health Visitor, writing her memoirs on the subject.

I took my leave of the earth and men,
And soared aloft to the lonely sky,
Thro' the gathering dark, to the silent stars,
And the whisper of Angels passing by.

I heard the beat of the Angels' wings,
In the silent watch of the starlit night.
I felt His touch, and I heard His Voice,
I, Man, communed with the Infinite.

Far below lies a burned-out wreck,
Soft, the strains of the bugle sound.
The Ensign flutters a last salute
As another pilot is laid to ground.

Men are sighing, and women weep.
Ah! Foolish friends, do not grieve for me,
For I heard God call in the silent night,
And flew on, into Eternity.

Molly Corbally
1913-2008

RAF – The Ancestors
Cecil Day-Lewis

When reviewing a new book on Day-Lewis in *The Telegraph* in 2007, Bevis Hillier wrote "Most educated people know three things about Cecil Day-Lewis: that he was Poet Laureate; that he joined the Communist Party; and that he was the father of Daniel Day-Lewis". Later when referring to Day-Lewis the man, he quotes one of the poet's most beautiful lovers, the novelist Elizabeth Jane Howard, as saying "I would defy any woman to resist him". Much has been written about this charismatic man whose poetic and literary output was colossal.

The last two lines of this poem are inscribed on the War Memorial to the Dallachy Strike Wing at Fochabers, Moray, Scotland. From Dallachy airfield RAF and Commonwealth squadrons flew Beaufighters and Mosquitos on anti-shipping strikes over the North Sea and along the Norwegian coast, depriving Germany of iron ore and other supplies, but at heavy cost. On one sortie alone, on 9th February, 1945, the wing lost nine aircraft.

Inventive men, haunted by images
Of Flight, they worked in power and stress to learn
The swallow's long endurance, the pacific
Gliding gulls, the plovers looping turn.

Audacious men, they clothed their vibrant vision
With wood and linen, flew it in the teeth
Of gravity, and like enchanters held
A fragile art between themselves and Death.

Air-worthy men, sons of the element
That speaks in light and lifts the venturer high,
They traced a buoyant span from shore to shore
Or fell like sunbursts from the embattled sky.

Their spirits rose in fine pitch off the field
Of earth, taking a steep way to the stars:
History flew beside them, and bright fame
Arches her wings above their cloudy wars.

Cecil Day-Lewis, CBE
1904-1972

The Battle of Britain
Cecil Day-Lewis

The citizens of London suffered appallingly from the day after day bombing of the blitz, but the Battle of Britain was fought thousands of feet above their heads and for most of them the only evidence of this desperate conflict were the con-trials left by the exhausts of the aircraft as they turned to ice crystals in the sub-zero temperatures, and the occasional trail of black smoke left by a fatally damaged German bomber or British fighter. But everyone knew, and relied upon, the courage of the young Allied pilots on whom the outcome of the battle depended.

What did we earth-bound make of it? A tangle
Of vapour trails, a vertiginously high
Swarming of midges, at most a fiery angel
Hurled out of heaven, was all we could descry.

How could we know the agony and pride
That scrawled those fading signatures up there,
And the cool expertise of them who died
Or lived through that delirium of the air.

Grounded on history now, we re-enact
Such lives, such deaths. Time, laughing out of court
The newspaper heroics and the faked
Statistics, leave us only to record.

What was, what might have been fighter and bomber
The tilting sky, tense moves and counterings;
Those who outlived that legendary summer;
Those who went down, it's sunlight on their wings.

And you, unborn then, what will you make of it –
This shadow-play of battles long ago?
Be sure of this: they pushed to the uttermost limit
Their luck, skill, nerve...

And they were young like you.

Cecil Day-Lewis, CBE
1904-1972

The Aeroplane
Gordon Boswell

Like Cecil Day-Lewis's poem on the previous page, Gordon Boswell's was written after watching dogfights from the streets of London during the Battle of Britain. This poem features on many aviation web-sites but sadly I can find no trace of the author.

I sweep the skies with fire and steel
My highway is the clouds,
I swoop, I soar, aloft I wheel
My engine laughing loud.
I fight with gleaming blades
The wind that dares dispute my path,
I leave the howling storm behind
I ride upon it's wrath.

I laugh to see your tiny world
Your toys of ships, your cars,
I rove an endless road unfurled
Where the milestones are the stars.
And far below, men wait and peer
For what my coming brings,
I fill their quaking hearts with fire
For death... is in my wings.

Gordon Boswell

The Submarine Hunters
F Scott Wills, 1941

F Scott Wills was a young pilot of 59 Squadron, Coastal Command who wrote this poem after his first operational flight over the Bay of Biscay in 1941 when the squadron was flying Bristol Blenheims and Lockheed Hudsons on anti-submarine duties. It captures perfectly the monotony of hours of search over the sea, seeking an elusive enemy.

No whale may blow, without our shrieking wings
Shall cleave the peace and drive her to the deep;
The goose turns swiftly from his arrow course;
The basking shark is troubled in his sleep;

While fingers numberless of dying wind,
Indolent, heedless, trailing on the swell,
Draw subtle, mystic lines into the haze –
Tell of the ancient silence we dispel –

No ship divides this never-ending sea
Which holds our eager eyes, as on a book
Of empty wordless volumes, page on page;
Hour upon hour, bewitched, we sit – and look –

Seeking the submarine, and seeing fish:
Swooping incredulous on porpoise play:
Looking for oil where beds of waving weed
Break the vast monotone of ocean grey:
Until, in reverie of search, our souls
Swim with the sea-gull-shrouded herring shoals.

F Scott Wills

Security
John Pudney

During war-time it has always been important for aircrew, in the event of their being shot down and taken prisoner, not to have anything on them that would help the enemy's intelligence services. To this end, before taking off on any flight, particularly one over enemy territory, all pockets had to be emptied.

This practice is still carried out by pilots who fly aerobatics lest anything dropping out of a pocket should jam the controls or be lost during an inverted manoeuvre.

Empty your pockets, Tom, Dick and Harry,
Strip your identity; leave it behind.
Lawyer, garage-hand, grocer, don't tarry
With your own country, your own kind.

Leave all your letters. Suburb and township,
Green fen and grocery, slip-way and bay,
Hot-spring and prairie, smoke stack and coal tip,
Leave in our keeping while you're away.

Tom, Dick and Harry, plain names and numbers,
Pilot, observer, and gunner depart.
Their personal litter only encumbers
Somebody's head, somebody's heart.

John Pudney
1909-1977

Combat Report
John Pudney

Every bombing mission had a briefing beforehand when aircrew were given the details of the target, navigation, weather etc., and crews were de-briefed immediately afterwards, usually in more sombre circumstances due to the absence of aircrew who did not return.

Fighter pilots were 'scrambled' at short or no notice and briefed in the air as they climbed towards the enemy. On return to base they submitted a combat report to the Squadron Intelligence Officer, claiming any victories over enemy aircraft. These were strictly regulated, requiring an independent witness to back up each pilot's claim. With adrenalin still flowing in their veins the young pilots could be in a quite excitable state when being de-briefed. As an intelligence officer Pudney would have listened to many of these reports.

Just then I saw this one come out.
You heard my shout? You, light and easy,
Carving the daylight. *I was breezy*
When I saw that one. O wonder,
Pattern of stress, of nerve poise, flyer,
Overtaking time. *He came out under*
Nine-tenths cloud, but I was higher.
Did Michael Angelo aspire,
Painting the laughing cumulus, to ride
The majesty of air. *He was a trier,*
I'll give this Jerry that. So you convert
Ultimate sky to airspeed, drift, and cover:
Sure with the tricky tools of God and lover.
I let him have a sharp four-second squirt,
Closing to fifty yards. He went on fire.

Your deadly petals painted, you exert
A simple stature. Man-high, without pride,
You pick your way through heaven and the dirt.
He burnt out in the air: that's how the poor sod died.

John Pudney
1909-1977

Air Gunner
John Pudney

Apart from weaving from side to side, at which they were lumberingly unsuited, the heavy bombers' only defences from fighters were their machine guns. These were in the charge of Air Gunners, usually non-commisioned officers, identifiable by their AG brevet supported by a single wing. They manned turrets in the nose, belly, upper fuselage, waist and tail of the four-engined bombers, usually firing multiple .303 or .5 inch guns. In tight formations the combined fire-power of these bombers was formidable and it took a brave fighter pilot to press home his attack.

The eye behind this gun made peace
With a boy's eye which doubted, trembled.
Guileless in the mocking light
Of frontiers where death assembled.

Peace was as single as the dawn,
Flew straightly as the birds migrating,
Timelessly in tune with time,
Purposeful, uncalculating.

So boyish doubt was put away:
The man's eye and the boy's were one.
Mockery and death retreat
Before the eye behind this gun.

John Pudney
1909-1977

Address to the Mother of a Dead Observer
Anthony Richardson

A dreadful responsibility of the Squadron's adjutant was to inform the next-of-kin of the death of a member of the Squadron and during war-time this would have been an almost daily occurrence. If the bereaved lived near to the Squadron's airfield a personal visit was always made. I defy anyone not to be moved by Anthony Richardson's poem which is one of several on this tragic theme in his small book of poetry entitled *Because of These – Verses of the Royal Air Force*, published in 1942.

Madam, this war is scarcely of my making –
Why pick on me? I'm sorry about Jack.
There was a gunner and a pilot, too,
Who won't come back...

I had to bring the news. It's just a part
Of an Adjutant's work. It breaks your heart?
Madam, I have no heart, I have none left –
So much bereft!

And can't you stop your wretched husband crying?
It's really rather trying.

That's right, sir. Pull yourself together, that's the 'gen' –
At least among men.
"*Poor bloody men...*" My wife said that,
When war broke out.

Madam, I frankly cannot see the use
Of treating me to your abuse.
I didn't kill your son. I gave no order
Posting him across the final border.
I'm only here to see if I can help...

Help? Stranger, what help could you give?
Can you make the dead live?

Once he grew within myself and lay
Wrapped in my body. Every night and day
He grew within me in that fast embrace,
Until at last I saw him face to face,
And he was in my likeness and I, aflame,
Cried out to God: "I glorify Thy Name."
And now God snaps his fingers...

Madam, I loved him too...
You owe me yet
Two shillings for the wire I sent his wife,
But that, alone, I'm willing to forget.

Flight Lieutenant Anthony Richardson, RAFVR

Luck
Dennis McHarrie

Wing Commander Dennis McHarrie, OBE, RAF was posted as a Flight Lieutenant to 38 Bomber Squadron, Middle East, in 1942, based at Barce near Benghazi. His poem echoes what many servicemen and women thought, that for all the heroic words that were written and said about their service and their sacrifices most of them went to war because they had no choice!

I suppose they'll say his last thoughts were of simple
 things,
Of April back at home, and the late sun on his wings;
Or that he murmured someone's name
As earth reclaimed him sheathed in flame.
Oh God! Let's have no more of empty words,
Lip-service ornamenting death!
The worms don't spare the hero;
Nor can children feed upon resounding praises of his deed.
"He died who loved to live," they'll say,
"Unselfishly so we might have today!"
Like hell! He fought because he had to fight;
He died that's all. It was his unlucky night.

Wing Commander Dennis McHarrie, OBE, RAF

Walking the Darkness
John Masefield

All that many of the population of southern England saw, or only heard, of the activities of RAF Bomber Command and the US 8th Air Force were the formations of bombers flying overhead on their way to targets all over continental Europe, mostly at night. John Masefield, Noel Coward and Sarah Churcill all captured the sight and sound of these great armadas, of which some 85,000* Allied airmen gave their lives during the Second World War.

Walking the darkness, far from home, at midnight,
Sometimes I see them, lighted at the wing-tips,
The cockpits winking with the spark of signals,
The out-bound bombers.

My thought perceives them switch away the sidelights
And cease to signal as they drive to danger,
From England, over sea, to blackened Europe
Where fire awaits them.

I say, 'O come home safely, midnight darers,
And may a day dawn when the youth of nations
Will hold like purpose, striving to make perfect
The life that binds us'.

John Masefield, OM. Poet Laureate
1878-1967

* RAF Bomber Command lost 55,000 men.
The US 8th Air Force lost 30,000 men.

Plastic Airman (For Sir Harold Gillies)
Wrenne Jarman

Like his cousin, that other great New Zealander and plastic surgeon, Sir Archibald McIndoe, Harold Gillies spent the war years rebuilding the faces and bodies of young men who were terribly disfigured by war, usually by fire. While McIndoe operated at East Grinstead, Gillies worked at Queen's Hospital for Facial Injuries in Sidcup, Kent.

Wrenne Madeleine Jarman – Renjie to her friends – was great-granddaughter of the poet Robert Millhouse. During the war she worked on a lathe at the Hawker Aircraft Works, Kingston and edited the Kingston News. Delicate but astonishingly beautiful, she died of cancer in 1953, aged 48. A collection of her poetry, entitled *Nymph in thy Orisons*, was published in 1961.

His face is smooth as sculptured faces are,
His features fair enough to draw a girl's
Arch backward glance, his disciplined blond curls
Swept from a grafted brow without a scar.

But this young mottled face does not betray,
As other faces do, the moods behind –
If he has secrets, they are locked away:
He looks out at the world from a drawn blind
Screening the man he was. And who was he?
Only the grave eyes know, and do not tell...

Be gentle with him, World, who has foregone
His unique pattern, his identity:
Be tender, lest the mask should melt
Abruptly, and surprise us with its scorn.

Wrenne Jarman
1905-1953

The Flying Instructor's Lament
Anonymous

Pilots will generally remember with affection the instructor/s who taught them to fly, although a few, if they did not get on with a particular instructor, would have been transferred to another. An Instructor's Rating is one of the advanced qualifications to which those who have a natural ability to teach, or who seek advancement in one of the flying services, will aspire.

During war-time many operational pilots were 'rested' with spells of instruction but there was a hard core of instructors who carried out the essential business of turning out pilots for the ceaseless demands of a service where losses were endless. This delightful doggerel from *Wings: An Anthology of Flight*, published in 1942, is a nice tribute to those essential men.

'What did you do in the war, Daddy?
How did you help us to win?'
'Circuits and bumps and turns, laddy,
And how to get out of a spin.'

Woe and alack and misery me! I trundle around the sky,
And instead of machine-gunning Nazis I'm teaching young hopefuls to fly;
Thus is my service rewarded, my years of experience paid,
Never a Hun have I followed right down nor ever gone out on a raid.

They don't even let us go crazy, we have to be safe and sedate,
So it's nix on inverted approaches, they stir up the C.F.I.'s hate.
For it's oh! Such a naughty example, and what will the A.O.C. think!
But we never get posted to fighters – we just get a spell on the Link.

So it's circuits and bumps from morning till noon, and instrument
flying till tea.
'Hold her off, give her bank, put your undercart down, you're
skidding, you're slipping' – that's me.
And as soon as you're finished with one course, like a flash up
another one bobs,
And there's four more to show round the cockpit and four more
to try out the knobs.

But sometimes we read in the papers of the deeds that old
pupils have done,
And we're proud to have seen their beginnings and shown them
the way to the sun;
So if you find the money and turn out the planes we'll give all we
know to the men
Till they cluster the sky with their triumphs and burn out the
Beast from his den.

NB C.F.I. – Chief Flying Instructor.
A.O.C. – Air Officer Commanding.
Link – The Link Trainer, an early flight simulator.

Anonymous

Flying Accident
Ian Rae

Ian Rae was a flying instructor during the Second World War, joining the RAF straight from school in 1942 and learning to fly in Canada. Although 'ab initio' flying training was still being carried out in the venerable Tiger Moth, the North American T-6, known as the Texan in America and the Harvard in Britain, became the advanced trainer later in the war. Rae published his book of poetry, *A Pilot's Notes*, in 2011, when he was 87.

I taught you how to fly.
There are few words that measure up to these
And yet it seemed you scarcely had to try,
Absorbing all that I could teach with ease.
We flew together on that final day
In sullen weather clearing from the west.
When through low cloud you climbed the Moth away
My feet were on the floor, my hands at rest.
You flew it, set the trim and throttled back,
Composed the flying speed, climbed straight ahead
Up through the scattered murk across our track
In silence, all my patter left unsaid.

Then suddenly the white and gold and blue
Of cloud and sun and sky were all around
Down on the dazzled tops our shadow flew
Wrapped in a little rainbow it had found.
Such is the brilliant kingdom of the few
Who cannot keep their feet upon the ground.

1st EDITION ISBN 1-84683-118-0

A PILOT'S NOTES

Poems of a World War Two Flying Instructor

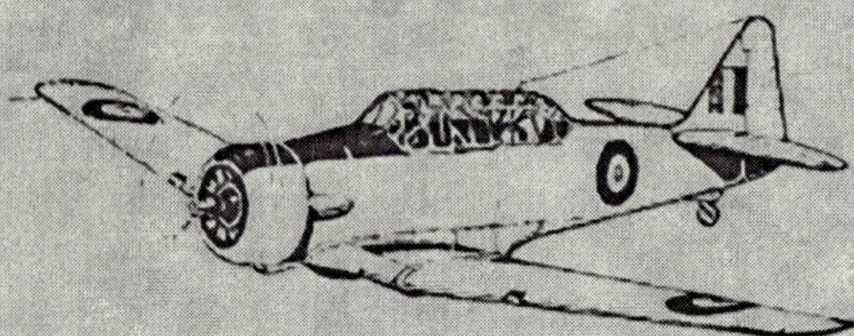

PREPARED BY DIRECTION OF THE MINISTER OF SUPPLY

PROMULGATED BY ORDER OF THE AIR COUNCIL

COMPOSED BY

Ian Rae

I knew your native skill was all your own
But I could build it, shape it, set it free.
We landed and I sent you off alone
To log an hour before we broke for tea.
Too soon they called me to the telephone.
The switchboard girl would only speak to me.

Well, there it is. I taught you how to fly
But you forgot one lesson. Or did I?

Ian Rae
1924-

Nuisance Raid
Ian Rae

Pairs of fighter-bombers regularly flew low-level sorties across the English Channel to take the war to the enemy. At first it was mainly the Luftwaffe making what were termed 'nuisance raids' but after the Battle of Britain it became the RAF's turn. Called 'rhubarbs', such raids were usually carried out from the airfields of Southern England. The Hawker Typhoon armed with rockets, and despite the unreliability of the Napier Sabre engine, was a favourite mount and the pilots were briefed to choose their own targets – trains being popular.

He came from France and brought a friend as well.
They crossed the Channel at a hundred feet.
We saw them circling Totnes, raising hell,
Then racing seawards with their task complete.

A few days later, buoyed by their success,
They brought their magic moments to Torquay.
This time the Bofors were at readiness
To drop them as they came in from the sea

Too smart for that, they crossed a quieter beach
A few miles north of us and tried
The oldest trick of tactics you can teach –
To hit the undefended, landward side.

Scoffins and I were watching fellows play
Some summer rugby on a seaside patch.
The first FW* that came our way
Seemed quite determined to abort the match.

He raked the pitch with tracer on his pass,
Players and watchers all were keeping down.
We watched the bullets race along the grass
Before he banked again towards the town.

Just at that point he took a fatal hit
Although we did not know of it at first.
This did not change his attitude a whit –
He thought he'd give us all another burst.

So just as we were thinking we'd retire
The German reappeared as if on cue.
From nose to tail the aircraft was on fire
But he was flying the thing and firing too.

He must have known that home was out of reach
And pulling up into a climbing turn,
He half-rolled, dived and hit the beach
Where for an hour or so we watched him burn.

A nuisance raid, the papers said next day.
We thought him brave and wished he'd got away.

* Focke Wolfe

Ian Rae
1924-

The Bomber
Beatrice Ruth Gibbs

It is not difficult to imagine the huge relief that the crew of a badly damaged bomber must have felt when they had successfully nursed their stricken machine across enemy territory, constantly under threat of further attack, and had crossed the English Channel to see the welcoming white cliffs of Dover, knowing that the massive runway at RAF Manston on the tip of Kent could take them if they could not make it back to base.

Born in Devon and educated at St. Margaret's school, Exeter and Sherborne School for Girls, Beatrice Ruth Gibbs became co-principal of Somerville School, St. Leonards, Sussex. This is another poem from Anne Powell's *Shadows of War*.

White moon setting and red sun rising,
  White as a searchlight, red as a flame,
Through the dawn wind her hard way making,
  Rhythmless, riddled, the bomber came.

Men who thought their last flight over,
  All hoping gone, came limping back,
Marvelling, looked on bomb-scarred Dover,
  Buttercup fields and white Down track.

Cottage and ploughland, green lanes weaving,
  Working-folk stopping to stare overhead -
Lovely, most lovely, past all believing
  To eyes of men new-raised from the dead.

Beatrice Ruth Gibbs
b.1894

Greatcoats
A J Burton

This, the last poem to be contributed to this anthology, came just in time to be included, from my old friend, retired Flying Officer Tony Haig-Thomas, who wrote about his RAF career in *Fall Out Roman Catholics and Jews* and is now Aviation Trustee of the famous Shuttleworth Collection at Old Warden in Bedfordshire. Tony keeps his extensive aviation library in his smallest room thereby encouraging his daily visits.

The poem was written on 7th July, 1943, by Pilot Officer A J Burton, of 103 Squadron, based at Elsham Wolds, who was reported missing on night operations five weeks later. Sent to the padre at Elsham by Burton's father, it was published privately in Air Marshal Sir Gareth Claytons' *...And Then There Was One* in 1985.

Hurriedly, carelessly, flung onto pegs
In the hall where the noise from the Mess filters through
Of the jokes of the crews over bacon and eggs
With no hint of the dangerous task they must do.

Like faithful old hounds with an eye on the door
The coats hang there quietly awaiting their men,
And twice must the airfield resound to the roar
Of engines before they are wanted again.

The sound of the last plane has died from the air
And the Mess is alive again to the din
Of cold hungry youngsters, yet warmly aware
Of another job done that is helping to win.

There is no lack of laughs yet a tiredness must creep
Into the eyes that have gazed on a city enflamed
So they eat, and are off to their billets to sleep,
But two or three coats hang there mutely – unclaimed.

Pilot Officer A J Burton RAF
Missing on operations, 1943

Lie in the Dark and Listen
Noel Coward, 1944

For almost three generations Noel Coward was one of the most prolific of English playwrights, composers, directors, actors and singers, and best known for his witty plays, musicals and songs. His poetry was probably the least of all his accomplishments but this fine tribute to RAF Bomber Command was written after he spent a night listening to massed bombers flying overhead on their way to Cologne in 1944. Adrian Swire sent me the first verse, one of the collection of writings in his flying log-book. The whole poem first appeared in *War Poems from The Sunday Times*, printed for private circulation in 1945.

Lie in the dark and listen.
It's clear tonight so they're flying high,
Hundreds of them, thousands perhaps,
Riding the icy, moonlight sky,
Men, machinery, bombs and maps,
Altimeters and guns and charts,
Coffee, sandwiches, fleece-lined boots,
Bones and muscles and minds and hearts,
English saplings with English roots
Deep in the earth they've left below.
Lie in the dark and let them go;
Lie in the dark and listen.

Lie in the dark and listen.
They're going over in waves and waves
High above villages, hills and streams,
Country churches and little graves
And little citizens' worried dreams;
Very soon they'll have reached the sea

Sir Noel Coward, 1899-1973

And far below them lie the bays
And cliffs and sands where they used to be
Taken for summer holidays.
Lie in the dark and let them go;
Theirs is a world we'll never know.
Lie in the dark and listen.

Lie in the dark and listen.
City magnates and steel contractors,
Factory workers and politicians,
Soft hysterical little actors,
Ballet dancers, reserved musicians,
Safe in your warm civilian beds,
Count your profits and count your sheep
Life is passing above your heads,
Just turn over and try to sleep.
Lie in the dark and let them go;
There's one debt you'll forever owe.
Lie in the dark and listen.

Sir Noel Coward
1899-1973

The Bombers
Sarah Churchill

Sarah Millicent Hermione Churchill was the second daughter of Sir Winston Churchill, Britain's wartime Prime Minister. She trained as an actress and dancer but during the war, while married to the comedian and singer Vic Oliver, she joined the Women's Auxiliary Air Force (WAAF), working on the interpretation of aerial photographs. After the war she starred in several films and also had her own television show. Divorced from Vic Oliver in 1945, she was twice re-married and twice widowed before dying in 1982 at the age of 67.

Whenever I see them ride on high,
Gleaming and proud in the morning sky,
Or lying awake in bed at night,
I hear them pass on their outward flight;
I feel the mass of metal and guns,
Delicate instruments, deadweight tons,
Awkward, slow, bomb racks full,
Straining away from downward pull,
Straining away from home and base,
And try to see the pilot's face,
I imagine a boy who's just left school,
On whose quick-learned skill and courage cool
Depend the lives of the men in his crew
And success of the job they have to do;
And something happens to me inside
That is deeper than grief, greater than pride,
And though there is nothing I can say,

I always look up as they go their way
And care and pray for every one,
And steel my heart to say,
"Thy will be done."

Sarah Churchill
1914-1982

Night Bombers
Anonymous

This is the fourth poem that I have selected on the theme of bombing. If that should seem monotonous and repetitious let it serve to represent the relentlessness of the Allied bombing campaign, initially carried out during daytime and then, when casualties by German fighters proved to be unacceptable, night after night after night.

Eastward they climb, black shapes against the grey
Of falling dusk, gone with the nodding day
From English fields.
                Not theirs the sudden glow
Of triumph that their fighter-brothers know;
Only to fly through cloud, through storm, through night
Unerring, and to keep their purpose bright,
Nor turn until, their dreadful purpose done,
Westward they climb to race the awakened sun.

Anonymous

Requiem for a Rear Gunner
R W Gilbert

Life for a rear-gunner, or Tail-end Charlie, as he was known in the RAF, was lonely, cold and dangerous. Anyone who has tried to get into the confined space of the tail turret of a Lancaster bomber knows that the prospects of getting out safely when the aircraft was damaged, and the occupant was heavily encumbered with flying gear and parachute, was practically nil.

This short poignant poem echoes the theme "They shall grow not old..." It appears in several places with different titles and attributions; I believe this title and author to be correct.

My brief sweet life is over
My eyes no longer see
No Christmas trees
No summer walks
No pretty girls for me
I've got the chop – I've had it
My nightly ops are done
Yet in another hundred years
I'll still be twenty one.

R W Gilbert

Raymond Baxter at RAF Laarbruch, 1976

Spitfire Special Delivery by Michael Turner
Fl Lt Raymond Baxter's Spitfire Mk XVI narrowly avoids a church spire as 602 Sqn make a precision low level attack on the V1/V2 headquarters in The Hague on 18th March, 1945
(by kind permission of the artist)

Air Thoughts Grounded
Raymond Baxter

Older readers will remember Raymond Baxter as the gravel-voiced television presenter and writer who was best known for being the first presenter of *Tomorrow's World*. He brought to his audience a rare enthusiasm for technical inventions with 'calm, measured tones and an old–school BBC voice' which equipped him well to be the radio commentator for such august ceremonies as the funerals of King George VI, Winston Churchill and Lord Mountbatten as well as the coronation of Queen Elizabeth II.

Not many knew that Raymond Baxter had a distinguished RAF war-time record, flying Spitfires with 65, 93 and 602 Squadrons. After the war he was employed by the BBC as outside broadcast commentator specialising in flying, motor cycling and motor racing, in many of which events he himself engaged while commentating. His most famous remark was when covering the first flight of Concorde; as the supersonic airliner left the ground for the first time he exclaimed: "She flies, she flies!"

His third gruelling tour in North Africa in 1943 so exhausted him that he had to spend two weeks recuperating in the RAF hospital in Ely, Cambridgeshire where this poem was written.

There is a world I deeply love,
And thither would I roam,
Where I can find true solitude
And be at peace alone.
And feel the living pulses
Of the thing they call "my kite",
The feeling of belonging
As part of it in flight.
Up where the air is clear as ice
In the realm of living light;

Where the silence is eternal,
Save for the song of flight.
There shimmering mountain masses rear
Their rounded heads in space;
And I would soar above them, turn
And dive upon them. Race
Along their clear cut canyons
With speeding, weaving ease,
Then bore into the hillside
Where swirling vapours freeze,
Blanketing the senses.
For I can spin the Earth before my eyes,
And throw it o'er my shoulder,
Because I love the skies!

These fancies flit before me
As I watch the patch of blue,
Framed by the ward's white window
Which is my prison view.
And I think of those I flew with,
Of those who fly no more,
Patrols and sweeps and "doggers-ho"
Above the fields of war.
The never-ending searching
Around the glaring skies:
The hunter or the hunted
Its he who has the eyes,
The skill, the nerve, the quickness,
And Lady Luck's sweet kiss,
It's he who lives to shoot the line
And claim his pretty miss!
But there is heart ache to it,
There's tragedy and fear!
But who recalls the horrors
When there's singing, and there's beer?
Yet when the songs are ended,
And there isn't any beer,

Come the shadows of the heart ache
And agony and fear,
Blanketing the glamour.
But I can spin the Earth before my eyes,
And toss it o'er my shoulder,
And still I love the skies.
Amen

Sqn Ldr Raymond Baxter, OBE
1922-2006

To a German Airman who flew slowly through the British fleet

Brian Gallie

Admiration for bravery by their opponents was shared by the Allies and Axis alike.

An Italian naval officer whose cruiser was torpedoed by a Swordfish from 830 Squadron based in Malta, for the rest of his life held that this was the bravest act he had ever seen. He asked his son to find the pilot's grave in England, to visit it and lay flowers there. His son finally paid this homage on his father's behalf in 2011.

Here a Royal Navy Captain records his admiration for a similarly brave opponent.

Perhaps you knew not what you did,
That what you did was good;
Perhaps the head I saw was dead,
Or blind with its own blood.

Perhaps the wings you thought you ruled,
With sky and sea beneath,
Beat once with love for God above –
And flew you to your death.

Perhaps: but I prefer to think
That something in you, friend,
No inch would give to land and live,
But conscious chose the end.

That something in you, like a bird,
Knowing no cage's bars,
Courage supreme – an instant dream
Of mind beneath the stars:

Misguided, arrogant, or proud,
But – beyond telling – great,
Made you defy our fire and fly
Straight on, to meet your fate.

Steel-capped, we cowered as you went,
Defiant and alone;
A noble thing, we watched you wing
Your way to the unknown.

You passed us, still a mile from death,
Rocked by the wind of shell:
We held our breath, until to death
Magnificent you fell.

Whatever comet lit your track –
Contempt, belief, or hate –
You let us see an enemy
Deliberately great.

Captain Brian Gallie, DSC, RN

A Fairey Swordfish of 820 Squadron over HMS Ark Royal
(Flight)

Illustration by Tugg
(By kind permission of The Willson Family)

The Stringbag Song
Anonymous

Bawdy songs have long been the prerogative of the sing-songs that follow mess dinners and there has never been a shortage of talented pianists in the services to pound out the accompaniment to songs which were never heard at home. If it follows that the more dangerous the service the more bawdy the songs, it is not surprising that the Fleet Air Arm's songs were the bawdiest! Until the 1960s the ratio of pilots lost from Royal Navy carrier operations was a shocking 1 in 3. Associated with the total absence of young ladies at sea (until the 1980s) and the liberal consumption of Horses' Necks and Pink Gins the result was unbridled bellowing of the songs contained in *The Fleet Air Arm Songbook*, a publication produced (For Private Circulation only) for its members by The Fleet Air Arm Officers Association and illustrated by the incomparable Tugg.

I was lent his copy by my old friend and recently retired Honorary Secretary of The Air Squadron, Simon Ames, OBE. Try as I might I could only find one song which would have passed the Lord Chancellor's scrutiny in the days when public decency was protected by that august office.

The much loved Fairey Swordfish, known as the 'Stringbag' because of its biplanes, laced fabric covering and interplane wires, was a stable but incredibly slow platform from which to launch aerial torpedoes, which it did with devastating effect at Taranto in 1940 and against the Bismark in 1941. The affection in which it was held was given full volume to the tune of "My Bonny Lies over the Ocean".

My Stringbag flies over the ocean,
My Stringbag flies over the sea,
If it wasn't for King George's Swordfish,
Where the hell would the Royal Navy be?

Chorus:
Stringbag, Stringbag,
Oh bring back my Stringbag to me, to me,
Stringbag, Stringbag,
Oh, bring back my Stringbag to me.

At Taranto and chase of the Bismark,
In the battle of Cape Matapan,
'Twas the fish from the Swordfish that fixed them,
And those who could run, how they ran!

Now the science of dropping torpedoes
Is taught at R.N.A.S. Crail,
Where the instruction's so good that pupils
With the Swordfish aren't likely to fail.

No doubt when we get Barracudas,
The Swordfish's day will be done,
So remember, 'twas this kite that fixed 'em,
And gave them their place in the sun!

Anonymous
c1943

Fleet Fighter
Olivia Fitzroy

Between 1943 and 1944 Olivia Fitzroy was a fighter direction officer in the Women's Royal Naval Service (WRNS) and served at the Royal Naval Air Station (RNAS) Yeovilton in Somerset, to this day the base for the Royal Navy's flying training. She was deeply affected by the deaths of her pilot boyfriend, killed near Singapore in 1945, and a WRNS girlfriend, killed in a car crash. After the war she lived in Wales and Scotland, becoming a prolific writer.

'Good show!' he said, leaned his head back and laughed.
'They're wizard types!' he said, and held his beer
Steadily, looked at it and gulped it down
Out of its jamjar, took a cigarette
And blew a neat smoke-ring into the air.
'After this morning's prang I've got the twitch;
I thought I'd had it in that teased-out kite.'
His eyes were blue and older than his face,
His single stripe had known a lonely war,
But all his talk and movements showed his age,
He had no thought but of the latest mod.
His jargon was of aircraft and of beer.
'And what will you do afterwards?' I said,
Then saw his puzzled face and caught my breath.
There was no afterwards for him, but death.

Olivia Fitzroy
1921-1969

For the Royal Air Force
John Masefield

England's unpreparedness for the Second World War was only just corrected in time, urged on by the oratory of Winston Churchill. Many private initiatives, such as Lady Houston's financing of the Rolls Royce engines that equipped the Supermarine Schneider trophy winners and developed into the world-beating Merlin, helped to redress the balance. In this tribute to the Royal Air Force Masefield captures the mood of those days before the United States of America came to Britain's aid.

You were as England when the war began,
  Unweaponed, helpless: but the Hope was yours
That the inhuman cannot beat the man,
  That devilry is tidal: right endures.

Thus confident, you fought, and fought alone.
  Often, at night, we heard you going by
And longed that you, bound outward, might come home
  Safe, from the fatal hells of foreign sky.

The hells are quiet now: a peace is ours.
  Whatever threatens us as peace begins,
We know that Brotherhood and Hope are powers,
  And you have shown that he who has them wins.

John Masefield, OM, Poet Laureate
1878-1967

Post-War
1945 Onwards

Introduction

After the euphoria of victory Britain had to face the cost of winning the war and the resultant austerity of the immediate post-war years. They were hardly times to re-inspire romantic poetry, and the novelty of aviation, if not flying, had long since disappeared. At the same time 'free verse' – verse without metre or rhyme – was becoming increasingly popular. Although I have included several examples in earlier sections I find that modern free verse lacks the inspirational quality of romantic poetry. Large amounts of unashamed doggerel from the period has been printed and although these produce a wry smile I find little to commend them to permanent record. For all three reasons the contribution from the 1940s and 1950s is disappointingly limited.

In the 1960s, and for the next fifty years, Man pushed his aeronautical frontiers out into space and a new age dawned but, despite wonderful photographs of the moon and the earth taken from space there was nothing in this highly technological new world, certainly on this side of the Atlantic, to inspire poetry.

However, there are still people, and importantly, young people, with aspirations to write poetry and I hope that those who experience the wonders of flight will commit to verse all the beauty and excitement that is still to be experienced in aviation today.

Lancasters
Audrey Grealy

The Avro Lancaster, designed by Roy Chadwick, was the most successful British heavy bomber of the Second World War. The prototype first flew on 9th January, 1941 and by the end of the war 7,377 Lancasters had been built. At the height of the bombing campaign against Germany the average life of a Lancaster on operations was just three weeks.

There is a lovely galloping rhythm to this down-to-earth poem by Audrey Grealy, whose husband was a Lancaster bomb-aimer flying a tour of operations with 12 Squadron, RAF, in 1943.

Where are the bombers, the Lancs on the runways,
Snub-nosed and roaring and black-faced and dour,
Full up with aircrew and window and ammo
And dirty great cookies to drop on the Ruhr?

Where are the pilots, the navs and air-gunners,
WOPs and bomb-aimers and flight engineers,
Lads who were bank clerks and milkmen and teachers,
Carpenters, lawyers, and grocers and peers?

Geordies and Cockneys and Wiltshire moon-rakers,
Little dark men from the valleys of Wales,
Manxmen, Devonians, Midlanders, Scouses,
Jocks from the Highlands and Tykes from the Dales?

Where are the Aussies, the sports and the cobbers,
Talking of cricket and sheilas and grog,
Flying their Lancs over Hamburg and Stettin
And back to the Lincolnshire wintertime bog?

Where are the flyers from Canada's prairies,
From cities and forests determined to win,
Thumbing their noses at Goering's Luftwaffe
And busily dropping their bombs on Berlin?

Where are the Poles with their gaiety and sadness,
All with the most unpronounceable names,
Silently, ruthlessly, flying in vengeance,
Remembering their homes and their country in flames?

Where are the Kiwis who left all the sunshine
For bleak windy airfields and fenland and dyke,
Playing wild Mess clinics like high cockalorum,
And knocking the Hell out of Hitler's Third Reich?

Where are they now, those young men of all nations,
Who flew though they knew not what might lie ahead,
And those who returned with their mission accomplished
And next night would beat up the Saracen's Head?

The Lancs are no more, they are now part of legend,
But memory stays bright in the hearts of the men
Who loved them and flew them through flak and through
  hellfire
And managed to land them in England again.

The men who were lucky to live and see victory,
The men who went home to their jobs and their wives,
The men who can tell their grandchildren with pride
Of the bomber which helped to save millions of lives.

Audrey Grealy
1922-

Little Stint

From Wikipedia, the free encyclopedia

The **Little Stint**, ***Calidris minuta*** (or *Erolia minuta*), is a very small wader. It breeds in arctic Europe and Asia, and is a long-distance migrant, wintering south to Africa and south Asia. It occasionally is a vagrant to North America and to Australia. It is gregarious in winter, sometimes forming large flocks with other *Calidris* waders, particularly Dunlin, on coastal mudflats or the edges of inland pools.

The numbers of this species (and of Curlew Sandpiper) depend on the population of lemmings. In poor lemming years, predatory species such as skuas and Snowy Owls take Arctic-breeding waders instead.

Its small size, fine dark bill, dark legs and quicker movements distinguish this species from all waders except the other dark-legged stints. It can be distinguished from these in all plumages by its combination of a fine bill tip, unwebbed toes and long primary projection. The call is a sharp "stit",

Non-breeding adult in Egypt

Flock in Andhra Pradesh, India.

The breeding adult has an orange wash to the breast, a white throat and a strong white V on its back. In winter plumage identification is difficult. Juveniles have pale crown stripes and a pinkish breast.

This bird nests on a scrape in bare ground, laying 3–5 eggs. It is polygamous, and male and female may incubate separate clutches.

Food is small invertebrates picked off the mud.

The Little Stint is one of the species to which the *Agreement on the Conservation of African-Eurasian Migratory Waterbirds* (AEWA) applies.

An apparent hybrid between this species and Temminck's Stint has been reported from the Netherlands.[2]

Little Stint

Adult in September

Conservation status

Extinct — Threatened — Least Concern

EX EW CR EN VU NT LC

Least Concern (IUCN 3.1)[1]

Scientific classification

Kingdom:	Animalia
Phylum:	Chordata
Class:	Aves
Order:	Charadriiformes
Family:	Scolopacidae
Genus:	*Calidris*
Species:	***C. minuta***

Binomial name

Calidris minuta

Leisler, 1812

Synonyms

Erolia minuta

Flying Machines
'Little Stint'

This delightful poem was sent to me by Roddy Blois, competition pilot extraordinary, who is so often flying all over the globe that one would be forgiven for thinking that he, like the Little Stint, is permanently migrating somewhere or other.

The Little Stint (*Calidris minuta* or *Erolia minuta*) is a very small migrating wader who breeds in arctic Europe and Asia and then flies thousands of miles to winter in South Africa, India and even Australia, visiting English shores on the way south in September and northward again during April to June.

For all Man's ingenuity and inventiveness he still cannot discover how migrating birds navigate and how this tiny life-form has the endurance to fly thousands of miles without rest.

I have been unable to identify the author who uses the pseudonym of the little long distance flyer but his doggerel delightfully captures the pathos of Man's short flirtation with aviation compared to the millennia of bird flight.

When Bleriot the Channel flew
The people made a great to-do.
They came in thousands just to stare
At the great Conqueror of the Air
Who crossed from France to England's shore,
A flight of twenty miles or more.
"How great an aeroplane!" they said;
"And what a noise the engine made!"
"And how could Bleriot know that he
Would find his way across the sea
Which none had ever flown before?"
And so they wondered more and more,
Until at last their hats they raise
And cheer to their great hero's praise.

Yet I, when called to make my flight,
Have slipped off in an Arctic night
And lightly flown o'er land and sea,
The only engine carrying me
My heart, no bigger than a shilling,
Which for twelve thousand miles is willing.
Less than two ounces is my weight,
No petrol cans increase my freight,
No chart nor compass 'neath my eyes
To mark the track through trackless skies,
And still untiring to the verge
Of Australasian ocean's surge.
From North Siberia's coast I fly
Spanning the globe unerringly.
No cheering thousands when I land,
No startling posters in the Strand;
No wondering word, no praise is heard,
But then – I only am a bird.

'Little Stint'

London – New York
Pamela Frankau

Only those who flew in the immediate post-war period, when airliners were unpressurised and still powered by piston engines, will remember the awful frustration of mechanical and weather related delays and diversions which could run into days and take the airliner to airfields far from their destination. Pamela Frankau, daughter of Gilbert Frankau (see page 85), wrote this wry parody of Rudyard Kipling's *Big Steamers* in 1948 after experiencing many transatlantic flights.

'Oh, where are you going to, all you big aircraft?
With tarmac and take-off, with instruments set...'
'We are going to drop you at Goose or at Gander,
in Scotland or Ireland; but don't ask us yet.'

'Still, could you come clean with me, all you big aircraft,
On the smallest of points that is causing me worry:-
Shall I be in New York at the time of your schedule?'
'This is highly improbable; what is your hurry?'

'Well, I'd like to explain to you, all you big aircraft,
That few people thrive upon sitting in space,
– no room for their legs, and their ears in discomfort –
unless they are certain of **getting** some place.'

'Why, then we have news of good cheer in abundance
for all who are anxious, who fret and who fuss.
If you'll kindly stop smoking, and fasten your seat-belts,
you'll find yourself back on the ground, thanks to us.'

'We have maintenance problems, electrical failures;
the weather's uncertainty now puts a ban on
our prudent advice to refuel at Gander.
Your safety comes first, so we're landing at Shannon.'

'And now we're aloft again, all you big aircraft,
flying North and not West, would opinion be right
in assuming America's out of the picture,
and we're therefore returning to Prestwick tonight?'

'My goodness, you passengers ask silly questions!
Our airspeed's terrific, our groundspeed's immense.
In less than two hours we shall be over Iceland,
so hush thee, my baby, and try to make sense.'

'Excuse me for troubling you, all you big aircraft,
But have we missed Iceland? And, if this be so,
can anyone tell me our time of arrival?
My friends were at Idlewild* four hours ago.'

'Just roll in your blanket and settle your pillow!
Our air-hostess radiates knowledge and charm.
She'll bring you some tea while we're passing the Azores,
so hush thee, my baby, we'll come to no harm.'

'I'm beginning to realize, all you big aircraft,
(nine-tenths of me wakeful, one foot sound asleep,
And my neighbour, a stranger, a log on my shoulder)
That the fares by Cunard are remarkably cheap.'

'Oh hush thee, my baby, no time to be peevish!
The port engine's heating, the ceiling is low...
We may have to circle around for a little.
*At the worst we can still get you back to Heath Row.'***

'For the route that you take, and the time that it takes you,
the hours that you waste and the places you visit,
– these are secrets kept from you by all us big aircraft,
and if that isn't proof of our kindness, WHAT IS IT?'

Pamela Frankau
1908-1967

*former name of John F Kennedy Airport, New York.

**now London Heathrow, the world's busiest international airport was originally named after the hamlet of Heath Row.

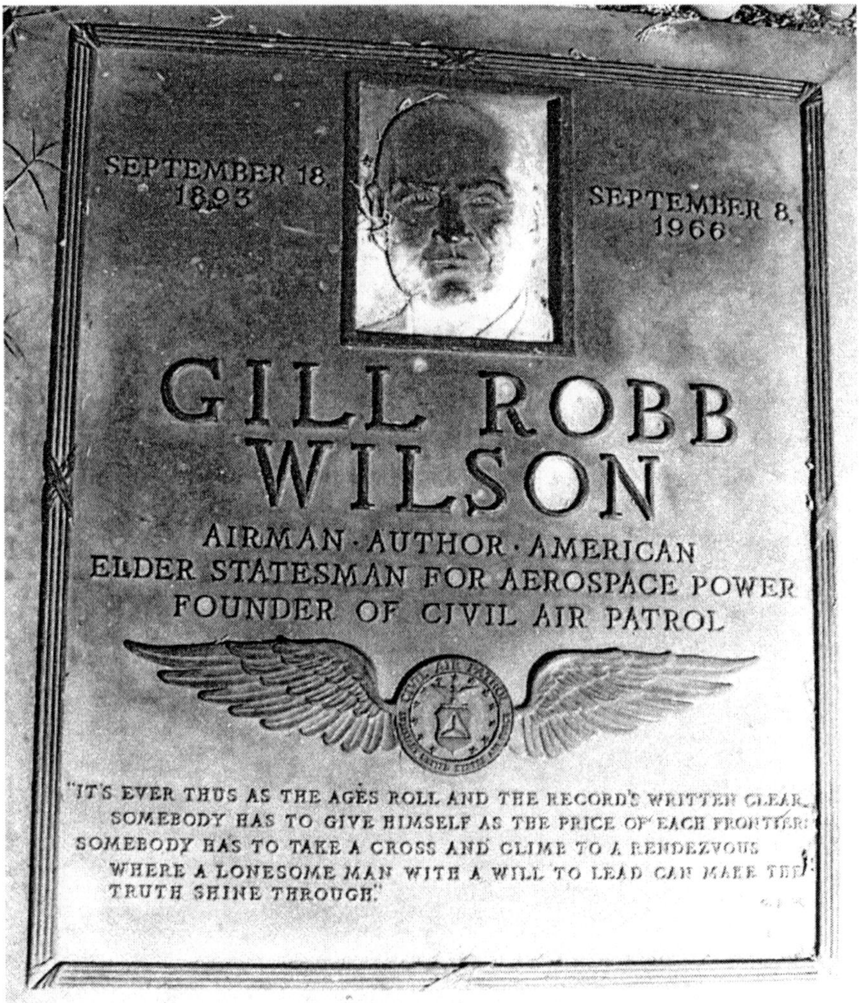

Gill Robb Wilson's memorial plaque in Forest Lawn Memorial Park (Covina Hills), Covina, Los Angeles County, California, USA

The Sunkissed Valley
Gill Robb Wilson

No anthology of aviation writing and poetry would be complete without examples of Gill Robb Wilson's beautifully written English. Gill was an American, the son of a Presbyterian minister who, with his brother, went to France in the First World War and drove ambulances, latterly becoming a member of the Lafayette Flying Corps with the French Escadrille Br.117. He subsequently became a minister of the Presbyterian Church but continued to be hugely active in aviation affairs, in 1930 becoming Director of Aeronautics for the State of New Jersey. With great vision for the future of civil aviation in America he became the first director of the Civil Air Patrol and then in 1939 the first member of the Aircraft Owners and Pilots Association (AOPA), now the world's largest general aviation organisation. He was an early editor of *Flying* magazine and wrote prolifically on the subject he loved – aviation.

This evocative essay from *The Airman's World*, published in 1957, was read by Sarah Hanna at the memorial services in St. Clement Danes for both her father, Ray, and her brother, Mark, and is another piece from Adrian Swire's log-book.

> You've been cruising the brooding hills under
> heavy skies – maybe a little lonely and a
> bit uncertain – when suddenly the westerning sun
> finds a slit in the canopy overhead.
>
> Long after you've forgotten the sweat of the journey
> you'll remember the glimpse of that sunkissed
> valley with the fingers of the hills all pointing
> to it as though fearful that you might
> miss its loveliness.

When you've flown enough years to have
crossed many hills and valleys, and known much
loneliness and endured many uncertainties – why then
you're a pilot, and on the walls of your memory
are hung such frescoes as no other breed of
man has ever seen. And because of them you can
never grow too old and you can never be too
much afraid of what lies ahead.

Just as the fact of flight telescopes time and space,
so the experience of flying telescopes the
pattern of life itself for the airman.

If you don't venture on sullen skies, you never
come to sun-kissed valleys. If your palms have never
been moist, your heart has never thrilled. If you
have never been afraid, you have never been courageous.

You have learned that if skies were always
cloudless, the hills and valleys beneath would be
barren. You have seen primordial forces at
work beyond the control of any man, but you have
fashioned a skill to live with them
in security and peace. You have sensed that where
there is no challenge there is no achievement.

So I think he learns of life, this one with the seven
league boots, this airman who goes from
place to place with such swiftness that even the
moods of the sky itself are
all caught up in his going and coming.

And if it does not mould him in humility of mind
and in peace of heart – and if he does not
become in spirit at one with the fingered hills
pointing eternally to some bright human hope which
nestles in the shadows of a sullen
history – then I have not read with understanding
for most of a lifetime the long, long thoughts
of my confreres – they who have earned a
citizenship in the airman's world.

Gill Robb Wilson
1892-1966

One of the Trusted
Gill Robb Wilson

The environment in which Air Transport works is so professional and regulated for the safety of the flying public that it is hard to conjure up romantic writings about it, but this is another piece of Gill Robb Wilson's free verse that is pure poetry and gives meaning to the old phrase 'a safe pair of hands'.

You are at cruising altitude
The westering sun is pink on the disc.
Your eye flicks the gauges. The engines are contented.
Another day – another dollar.

You look down at your hands on the wheel.
They are veined and hard and brown.
Tonight you notice they look a little old.
And, by George, they are old. But how can this be?
Only yesterday you were in flying school.
Time is a thief. You have been robbed.
And what have you to show for it?
A pilot – twenty years a pilot – a senior pilot.
But what of it – just a pilot.
Then the voice of the stewardess breaks in on your reverie.
The trip is running full – eighty-four passengers
Can she begin to serve dinner to the passengers?
The passengers – oh yes, the passengers.
You noticed the line of them coming aboard –
The businessmen, the young mothers
with the children in tow, the old couple,
the two priests, the four dog-faces.

A thousand times you have watched them
file aboard and a thousand times disembark.

They always seem a little gayer after the landing
than before take-off. Beyond doubt
they are always somewhat apprehensive aloft.
But why do they continuously come up here?
in the dark sky despite their apprehension?
You have often wondered about that.
You look down at your hands again
and suddenly it comes to you.

They come because they trust you –
you the pilot. They turn over their lives
and their loved ones and their hopes and dreams
to you for safekeeping.
To be a pilot means to be one of the trusted
They pray in the storm
that you are skilful and strong and wise.
To be a pilot is to hold life in your hands –
to be worthy of faith.
No, you have not been robbed.
You aren't "just a pilot". There is no such thing
as "just a pilot". Your job is a trust.
The years have been a trust.
You have been one of the trusted.
Who could be more?

Gill Robb Wilson
1892-1966

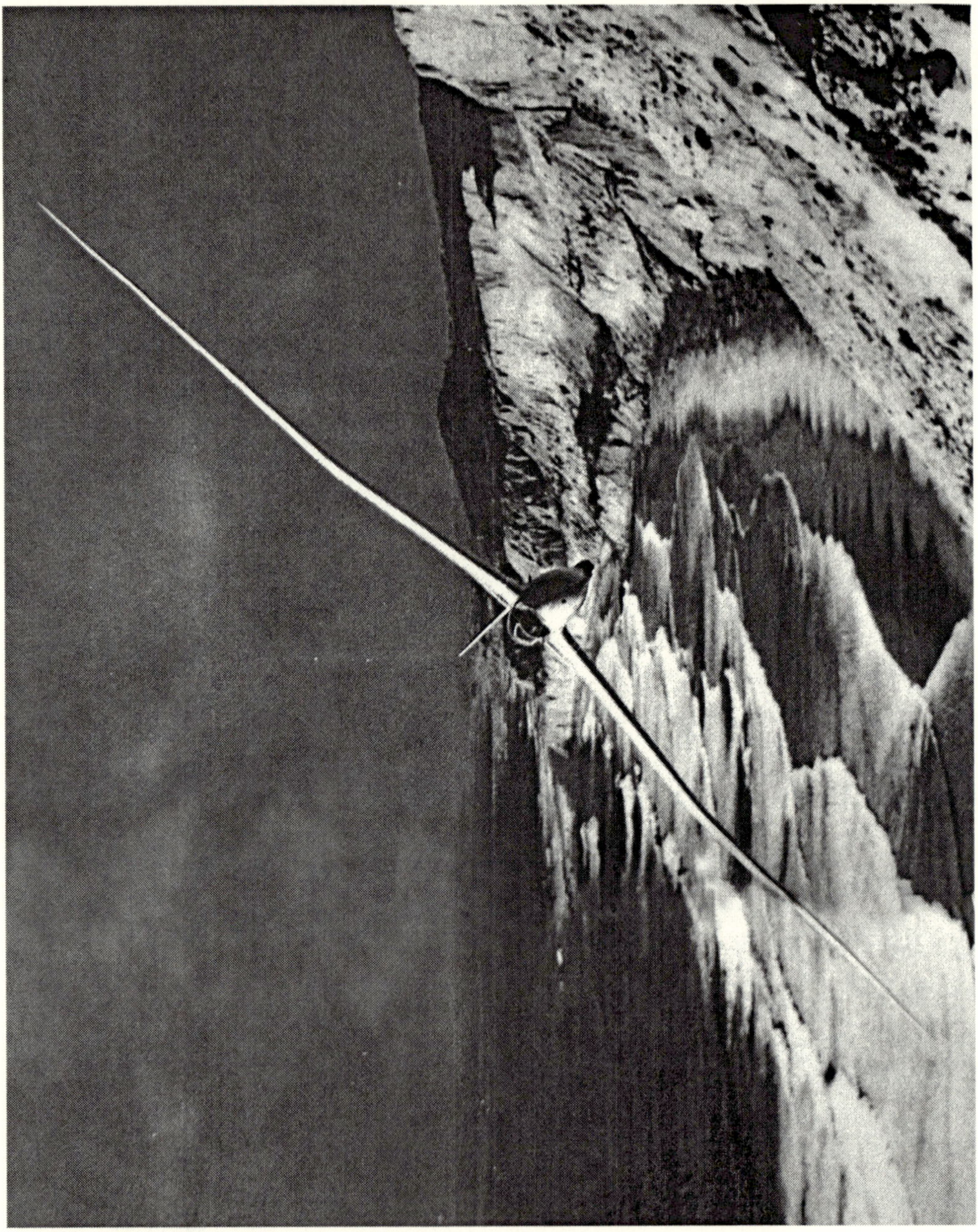

Don Downie

The Sailplane
Gill Robb Wilson

Here is another poem from Gill Robb Wilson in which you can almost hear the silence of gliding!

Where the lace of the waters is stitched to the land
by the throb of the tide in the sea,
and the earth in erosion lends scallops of sand
to ruffle the surf that is hemmed to the land –
the fingering zephyrs will be.

And here in the atmosphere's ambient change
and the local effect of the continent's range,
the sailors who sail on the ocean of air
with naught but their knowledge to carry them clear –
assemble their sensitive planes.

What is formed in the instinct of gull and of tern
by the cunning of nature, the sailor must learn,
and the art is less matter of knowledge to fly
than of being at home with the moods of the sky –
and patience to learn.

Here, absent the surge and the roar of the screw
and advice from the tower and the help of a crew;
here only the lisp of the waves on the sand
and the whisper of zephyr upswept from the land –
and your art and you.

Gill Robb Wilson
1892-1966

"Me miserable! Which way shall I fly...?"
Satan, as drawn by Gustav Dore, in John Milton's Paradise Lost

Me Miserable! Which Way Shall I Fly...?
T E Johnson

This title, from John Milton's *Paradise Lost*, and the two clever parodies of Milton's *L'Allegro* and *Il Penseroso* were written by Flight Lieutenant TE Johnson, DFC, while he was on the Standardisation Flight, No. 6 FTS, Ternhill, under the following introduction,

> Since 1939-45 the training given a service pilot has undergone considerable change. That this should be so is understandable since flying has become so complex an affair. But although the flying instructor should have a good knowledge of the theory of flight and aerodynamics as a background to his job, it does not follow that the pupil, when first learning to fly, needs to probe, say, the mathematics of lift. There is ever the danger that the theoretical may assume more importance than the practical. Perhaps then, to those who instruct, the following parody, with apologies to John Milton, will serve as a reminder of the change (a bit exaggerated, it might be) which has taken place.

L'Allegro – 1939 – 1945

Haste thee Lad, and bring with thee
Thy parachute – sweet Liberty –
And helmeted we'll see what doth
Lift and control the Tiger Moth.
This prop to pull, these wings to lift,
And cables twain lest one should rift,
This tail plane, rudder, and cockpit
- The front is where I'm going to sit –
Will soon be yours to fly alone,
Which mysteries are now unknown.

Straight your eye will catch new pleasures
As new angles landscape measures;
Russet lawns and ploughland bare,
All passed over in the air.
Then for joy, like eagles stoop,
Dive and climb and loop the loop:
Stick back! Wings straight! There he flies,
The cynosure of neighbouring eyes.

Sometimes with secure delight
We'll spin and let it wind up tight.
First the rudder: then the stick:
Still full rudder . . . Now then quick
See the spin stop? Centralize,
And ease out of the resultant dive.
Now let's climb again and see
You use full rudder . . . not just me.

And ever against aching care
Perfect all movements in the air.
Try and try; then try again:
Co-ordination be your aim.
Never do too low gyrations,
Till you know your limitations.
Then you'll find there's nothing in it
If you stay within your limit.

All these hints and tips I give
Will help you fly, and fight, and live.

Il Penseroso – 1945 – 195?

Now Pupil have you read the Data
In the Notes? You've not? Well later
When the Prentice book you've studied,
Through the One Two Nine you've hurried,
Come to me, and we will talk.
I will show you with the chalk
On the blackboard, how the lift
Varies, and how sideways drift
Occurs with every beam wind blowing.
...But hurry now! Be up and doing!

Come Pensive Pupil, you believe in
Errors which this per-flight briefing
Should dispel. First now the graphic
Form of lift which is not static
But which rises to a peak or
Critical angle, then gets weaker.
On the co-efficient number,
Or on Reynolds, you may blunder,
So be sure you pay attention:
New ideas cause such dissention.

Oft, on a plot of rising ground
You may hear jet engines sound:
But they are not for you. Oh no!
Those pilots all know what is rho,
And how the lift equation looks
When written in their little books.
You Pupil, have a lot to learn,
For instance. why the slipstreams turn:
Induced flow: vortices and that
Elusive boundary layer: Mach:
And if you never learn to fly,
At least you'll learn the reason why.

And may at last your weary age
With Kermode, Pearcy, and the sage
Aerodynamicists find rest,
That you can speak out with the best.
'Tis certain you will not feel sane
While working problems in a plane:
So if you want the answer right,
Not airborne ...on the ground sit tight!

These problems Melancholy give,
And I with thee will choose to live.

Flight Lieutenant TE Johnson, DFC, RAF

An Old Airfield
Ian Rae

Hundreds of airfields were constructed all over Britain prior to, and during the Second World War, mostly in East Anglia because of their proximity to Germany. Some of these still exist as active airfields, lengthened and modernised to take the jet aircraft of the Royal Air Force and the United States Air Force.

Some have disappeared completely, but there are many which can be identified, particularly from the air, by their concrete dispersal areas, taxiways and runways, partly demolished and mostly surrounded by encroaching farmland. One can only guess what goes through the mind of a veteran airman who returns to visit his old base, once the scene of such intense aviation activity.

Glimpsed from the road through upstart conifers
With pink-splashed rhododendrons on its rim,
A concrete disc resists the spreading wood.
This old dispersal point makes fifty years
Vanish like fifty seconds as I scan
These rough, flat acres stretched towards the sea.

The taxi track remains, a few black huts,
A square control tower, boarded up and blind
To that long runway it commanded once.
A great wide road devoid of purpose now,
Whiskered with weeds, coarse grasses bursting out
Through every crack and softening every edge.

How still this place is. Only drifting gulls
Cry listlessly above the airfield now
Where once the noisy squadrons coughed to life,
Growling and rumbling to the runway's end.
A pause, a wave, a green light flickering,
Then silhouettes slow-climbing to the east.

You must have guessed I meant to come this way.
Now, sensing ghosts, I do not wish to stay.

F/O Ian Rae, RAF
1924-

Bomber County

Audrey Grealy

The skies are empty now as darkness falls
The bare deserted runways scarred with weeds
Across the lonely fen a night bird calls
The wind sighs softly in the whispering reeds.

A fitful moon rides through the cloudy blue
A bomber's moon, remembered now no more
Where once the very air vibrated to
The mighty Merlin engines' throbbing roar.

Dispersal huts stand crumbling and forlorn
Their broken windows open to the rain
The taxi track is fringed with waving corn
The echoing hangars used for storing grain.

Upon the cracking tarmac wander sheep
A derelict crew-room door creaks in the breeze
The silent world around is lost in sleep
And stars are twinkling far above the trees.

Those very stars which were a friendly aid
To those who flew upon the wings of night
The crews who never grudged the price they paid
To keep aglow the flame of freedom's right.

There is no flarepath now to show the way
And guide the homing bombers to the ground
The old control tower stands in gaunt decay
In silence and in darkness wrapt around.

Remember those who flew, across the years
Those bright young lives they gave so long ago
No looking back with bitterness or tears
But thankfulness – for they would wish it so.

Audrey Grealy
1922-

One Sunday Afternoon at Redhill
Arthur Golding-Barrett, circa 1965

This poem appeared in the *Tiger Rag*, the monthly news-letter of The Tiger Club, which was the crucible of sporting flying in England between the 1950s and 1970s. (It is still flying out of Headcorn aerodrome in Kent). The poem was ascribed to 'G-B', Wing Commander Arthur Golding-Barrett, one of the founding fathers of the Club (the others being Norman Jones, the owner of the club and all its aeroplanes, and 'Bish', CA Nepean-Bishop, a legendary instructor on Tiger Moths.)

G-B was a silver haired 60-something year old who was mother-hen to all the young pilots of the Tiger Club. Because he was over twice our age he was ribbed unmercifully by us – which he took in great good humour – but many took their troubles to G-B when they couldn't sort them out themselves.

If he did write this poem it is a worthy tribute to his devotion to the Tiger Club and its members. It captures perfectly the spirit of the week-end flyers at Redhill, the club's base in Surrey, and most certainly reflects G-B's feelings for his young charges.

They stand there, in the splendour of their youth,
Mocking at life, at love, at age, at truth,
Fully alive, the present all their need,
Today a certain now, tomorrow not their heed.
Then, on a hidden impulse not defined,
Breaks up the group, each on his own inclined
To other meetings or a chosen task
Is now unfettered, that is all they ask.
From factory bench or office desk they come
From Stock Exchange or counter every one
Escapers all from hum-drum workday role
To find in flying that which makes them whole.

G-B and admirer at Redhill, 1964
(Author's photograph)

G-B briefs the author on the finer points
of flying a Tiger Moth, 1963
(Author's photograph)

In phrases strange, staccato, fierce and slick
They talk of 'G' and rate of roll, or flick,
Of Cuban 8s, inverted systems, knots,
Positioning, of spins, of CSUs and slots.
Another, arms in curving gesture shows
How his own aerobatic sequence goes.
Oblivious to all, yet man to man,
They argue, change, consolidate their plan.
And in a trice to put it to the test
Are in the air, relentless in their zest.
To loop and spin, stall turn and 8-point roll
Nought else in mind, perfection all their goal.
And some of us who stand enthralled, aghast,
Bemused by memory of flying days long past,
When we, like them, were young and gay and bold
And laughed like them at others then grown old,
Recall and yearn to tell, and yet stay mute,
Afraid – (for age can't always talk to youth,)
Nor dare to criticise and never blame.
We had so much – they'll never have the same.
So now they fly while we no longer young
Muse on the past and long to join the fun,
Politely shunned – we've had our share of time,
Our flying lives now spent, we're past our prime.
But years before, we realise with dismay,
Did we pay homage? No! So why should they?

Wing Commander Arthur Golding-Barrett
1904-1976

The Unkindest (Defence) Cut of All
Harry C Heyward

This clever and witty poem came to me from Chief of Air Staff, Air Chief Marshal Sir Peter Squire, veteran of the Falklands conflict where he won a DFC flying Harriers off HMS Hermes as CO of 1(F) Squadron. Originally written during the early nineties when the then Conservative government sought to take the 'peace dividend' and axed the RAF front-line squadrons by thirty-eight percent, there have since been several variants. I have nevertheless ascribed this one to the original author.

Once again another Conservative government is dramatically reducing the armed forces and no doubt another author, imbued with that admirable English trait that comes to the fore in dire times – bloody-mindedness and a sense of humour – will produce a 'final' version.

I'm the last man left in the Air Force
I've an office at MOD
And a copy of Queen's Regulations
Which only apply to me.
I can post myself to Leuchars
And detach me from there to Kinloss
Or send me on courses to NATO
Then cancel the lot. I'm the boss.

I'm the last man left in the Air Force
I suppose you imagine that's great
To be master of all you survey, but
I tell you it's difficult, mate
I inspected three units last Thursday
As C-in-C (Acting) of Strike
Then I cleaned out the bogs at Brize Norton
And repaired Saxa Vord's station bike.

I'm the last man left in the Air Force
My wife says I'm never at home
When I'm not flying kites I'm at Manston
Laying gallons and gallons of foam
Or I'm in my marine craft off Plymouth
Shooting flares at the crowds on the Hoe
Or I'm orderly corporal at Luqa
It's an interesting life but all go.

I'm the last man left in the Air Force
I'm ADC to the Queen
I'm duty clerk at St Mawgan
I'm the RAF Rugby team
Tomorrow I'm painting the guardroom
And air testing several planes
The day after that I'm in London
To preach at St. Clement Danes.

I'm the last man left in the Air Force
And I'm due to go out before long
There's been no talk of any replacement
And I won't even let me sign on
I hope to enjoy my retirement
I've put up a fairly good show
But I won't cut myself off entirely
There's always reunions you know.

Harry C Heywood, W/O, TCC, Grimsby

Sea Harriers line the deck of HMS Hermes as she leaves Portsmouth for the Falklands in April, 1982

By kind permission of David Morgan

Thoughts of Home
David Morgan

David 'Mog' Morgan's career in the Royal Navy nearly ended ignominiously when he was 'chopped' from helicopter flying in 1968. He transferred to the Royal Air Force the subsequent year, flying Wessex helicopters and then Harriers. Posted on exchange to the RN to fly the Sea Harrier (SHAR), he was one third of the way through this course when the Falklands War started and he sailed to the South Atlantic in HMS Hermes with 800 Naval Air Squadron.

Mog's father had been a Fleet Air Arm Seafire pilot in WW2 with one German and two Japanese aircraft to his credit. After the war he became a teacher and introduced his son to John Pudney's verse, a copy of which he had carried with him throughout the war. Much influenced by Pudney and others Mog wrote romantic poetry as a release for his emotions while serving in Northern Ireland and the Falklands .

A million care-worn miles it seems
Away from England's crystal streams
And shady meadows, nestling there
With flags and daisies in their hair.
Decked all about with opal pine
Parade of hedgerows in a line.

From lilac-perfumed evenings, cool
With dew, beside love's languid pool
Where laughed and dreamt we both, as one,
Warmed by the soul's remembrance of the sun.
Our hearts with roses close entwined
In soft and scented summer wind.

Flight Lieutenant David Morgan, DSC, RAF

A hundred well remembered years
Of laughter, love and childhood's tears,
And shouts of joy from boys and girls
With life's bright radiance in their curls.
Few thoughts of anger, strife or pain
Eclipsed the sun of that domain.

Ten thousand glorious days with you
Mid blazing autumn's lustrous hue.
Those summer nights when dawn drew nigh
To find us nestled thigh by thigh
With arms entwined. So soft we lay,
In awe, to greet the birth of day.

And yet, across wide time and space
I swear I oft-times see your face
And feel your arms about me, when I fly
Across this alien, Southern sky.
And sometimes catch sweet lilac's smell
Above the stench of Mars's hell.

Fl Lt David Morgan, DSC, RAF
1947-

DAVID MORGAN
HOSTILE
SKIES
'MY FALKLANDS AIR WAR'

Der Traum (The Dream)
David Morgan

Despite his unfamiliarity with SHAR Mog proved to be a most successful fighter pilot, shooting down four enemy aircraft and, unusually for an RAF officer, being awarded the RN's Distinguished Service Cross. He wrote of his experiences in the Falklands in *Hostile Skies*, a fine balance to the more flamboyant Commander "Sharky" Ward's *Sea Harrier over the Falklands*. Finally transferring back to the RN in 1984, he was placed on the retired list in 1992 and is now a long-haul Captain with Virgin Atlantic and, in his spare time, a display pilot.

Oh how you laughed that day,
The wild wind tugging at your hair.
The warm west wind that bore
Our surging steed into the air.

And how we soared and vaulted
Through those azure skies
Our hearts a song, as fast as light
We far outflew the seagulls' cries
And lost ourselves within our hearts' desire.

Then down we came, our souls
Alight with fire and wonder
At the beauty of our flight.

And as you jumped down from the wing
You said,
"Kiss me"

Fl Lt David Morgan, DSC, RAF
1947-

Mark Hanna flying Spitfire Mk IX MH434

Ray Hanna about to fly P51 Mustang 'Big Beautiful Doll'

You Love A Lot of Things...
Ernest Hemingway

I include this motto of The Old Flying Machine Company, founded by Ray Hanna and based at the historic airfield of Duxford in Camridgeshire, as a tribute to Ray and his son Mark for their years of wonderful display flying, mainly on Spitfire IXb, P40E Kittyhawk, P51D Mustang and FG-I D Corsair, and because Ray checked me out on his Mark IXb Spitfire MH434, then belonging to Adrian Swire, for one glorious flight in 1970.

Although Hemingway wrote much on aviation and was passionate about flying he was, strangely, never a pilot himself.

"You love a lot of things if you live around them, but there isn't any woman and there isn't any horse, not any before, nor any after, that is as lovely as a great airplane. And men who love them are faithful to them even though they leave them for others. A man has only one virginity to lose in fighters, and if it is a lovely plane he loses it to, there his heart will ever be."

Ernest Hemingway

Impressions of a Pilot
Gary Claude Stoker

This poem was recently read at the funeral service of Air Chief Marshal Sir Christopher Moran KCB, OBE, MVO, ADC, C-in-C Air Command, who died suddenly of a heart attack in May, 2010 at the age of 54. At the time of writing I have been unable to trace any record of the author.

Flight is freedom in its purest form,
To dance with the clouds that follow a storm;
To roll and glide, to wheel and spin,
To feel the joy that swells within.

To leave the earth with its troubles and fly,
And know the warmth of a clear spring sky;
Then back to earth at the end of the day,
Released from the tensions which melted away.

Should my end come while I am in flight,
Whether brightest day or darkest night;
Spare me no pity and shrug off the pain,
Secure in the knowledge that I'd do it again.

For each of us is created to die,
And within me I know,
I was born to fly.

Gary Claude Stoker

Flight
Prunella Power

In 1934, at the age of only 20, Prunella Power (nee Stack) took over the Women's League of Health and Beauty after the death of her mother who had founded it; she was known as Britain's 'Perfect Girl'. In 1938 she married Lord David Douglas-Hamilton, youngest son of the 13th Duke of Hamilton, and gave birth to her first son Diarmaid in 1940, and her second son Iain, in 1942.

David achieved the rank of Squadron Leader in the RAF; his three brothers made Air Commodore, Group Captain and Wing Commander. David commanded 603 (City of Edinburgh) Squadron flying Spitfires out of Malta in 1941/42 but was killed when his heavily shot up Mosquito crashed when returning from a reconnaissance flight over France in 1944. In 1950 Prunella married a surgeon, Alfred Albers, who tragically fell to his death while climbing Table Mountain; they had been married just nine months. With her third husband, Irish barrister Brian Power, she bought a croft on the island of Raasay, off Skye, where she wrote poetry and her autobiography. She died on December 30th, 2010, aged 96.

This very English sonnet must have been written by Prunella after a flying experience although she herself never learned to fly.

> Poised on the runway, eager as you are
> to be released into the arching* sky,
> vibrating with the engine's growing power
> skimming the ground, then taking off to fly
> You're one now with another element
> where citadels of clouds will welcome you
> and earth below become a childish tent
> forsaken for this all-embracing blue.
> Pulsing ahead, your engine's steady hum
> is background to the music of the spheres

Lord David Douglas-Hamilton holds up his nephew, the Marquis of Clydesdale, to see his cousin Diarmaid, held by his mother, Lady Douglas-Hamilton, the former Miss Prunella Stack

unheard below, but here the precious sum
of freedom and release from human years.
How can I bear to bring you back to earth
when we have shared this magical re-birth?

*an amendment in the author's hand changes the word 'arching' to 'furthest'.

Prunella Power, OBE
1914-2010

Squadron Leader Lord David Douglas-Hamilton, 1912-1944

On Looking into a Pilot's Operational Log-Book, 1941-1944
Prunella Power, 24.11.1979

A pilot's log-book is the truest source of information about his flying career; a unique diary of every flight he ever made, and as such an invaluable possession. It is not difficult to imagine the poignancy with which a Royal Air Force widow would read this personally handwritten record of her late husband's operations right up to his final flight; experiences about which pilots rarely spoke to their loved ones.

And is there any time I could forget
you, the first and fairest,
you, the rarest
scornful of lies
you, with the brave heart
and proud eyes?

Day after day
I watched you part
your load too hard for words
so, lacking words
I tended, soothed, unmasked,
and never asked.

In thirty years
I don't forget your hand
your d, your l, they tell
your hopes your fears
your sorties through the flak
your long way back
even your last failure to land.

All, all are here
though never said
the words speak clear
I hear
the sad tongue of the dead.

Prunella Power, OBE
1914-2010

The four sons of the 13th Duke of Hamilton
From left to right: David, Squadron Leader, 1912-1944;
Douglas, Air Commodore, AFC, 1903-1973;
Geordie, Group Captain, AFC, 1906-1994;
Malcolm, Wing Commander, OBE, DFC, 1909-1964

Operational Log-Book
Prunella Power, 17.1.1980

Just two months after writing *On Looking into a Pilot's Operational Log-Book*, Prunella Power wrote *Operational Log-Book* on the same theme.

After the sorties you wrote them down
swift, informative factual word –
"bounced by MEs* out of the sun" –
And here's the story I never heard.

Red of pain, yellow of fear,
Black of dread should stain the page,
Yet all I see is your writing, clear,
But greying now with the colour of age.

And why should secrets long untold
(dazzle of danger, sky at dawn,
Lurch of heart as the chances fold)
Matter now when so much has gone?

And yet, and yet, your D, your I,
(dear as the hairs on your fallen head)
Speak to me. They tell, they tell
The truth that never could be said.

Prunella Power, OBE
1914-2010

* Messerschmitts, probably BF109s

Lord David Douglas Hamilton about to fly his wife Prunella, aged 27, in a Mark II Spitfire in 1941

Diarmaid Douglas-Hamilton about to fly his mother Prunella, aged 86, in a Cessna 172 in 2000

(Photographs by kind permission of Diarmaid Douglas-Hamilton)

New England
Prunella Power

While a Squadron Leader in the Royal Air Force, David Douglas-Hamilton had, against all regulations, flown his wife Prunella in a Spitfire, a thrilling experience for both of them! To achieve this in the single seat fighter, he sat her first in the cockpit with her legs dropped either side of the seat, and then he squeezed himself in front of her, sitting between her thighs, which gave him just enough space to handle all the controls.

In 2000 Prunella was flown in a light aircraft from Beverley, Massachusetts, to Bethel, Maine by her elder son, Diarmaid Douglas-Hamilton. The flight reminded her of her clandestine Spitfire flight fifty-eight years earlier.

A rush of air
As the small plane lifts,
Your capable hands
Shaped like your father's
Grasping the stick,
My stomach lurching
The years cart-wheeling
And yes, I remember.

Forbidden flight
Squeezed into a Spitfire
The RAF Station
Unrolling below us.
His hand on my shoulder
Bitter-sweet warning
Of hazards to come
In France and Malta.

And now with you
Above New England,
The new and the old
In familiar pattern.
The plane banks steeply
And sharp as hail,
I know beyond doubt
Time is no healer.

Prunella Power, OBE
1914-2010

Sky Fever
Martin Barraclough, 2006

By flying his Gipsy Moth across the Tasman Sea and to Japan during the late 1920s, and rebuilding it himself every time he crashed it, Sir Francis Chichester acquired fame as an aviator and navigator long before he sailed *Gipsy Moth IV* around the world. He took the title of his autobiography, *The Lonely Sea and the Sky*, from the first line of John Masefield's *Sea Fever* which he describes as giving "in only twelve lines the key to my life-time search for romance and adventure".

Several pilots have parodied Masefield's great poem including myself and I offer mine here, with apologies to the late John Masefield, and the late Sir Geoffrey de Havilland whose autobiography bears the same title.

I must take off for the skies again, to a lonely deep blue sky,
And all I ask is a pair of wings and the power that makes
them fly,
And a stick in my hand, the sun on my face and the flying
wires humming,
And the land below moving steadily by, and a horizon
coming.

I must take off for the skies again, for the call of flying high
Is a stern call and a clear call that I cannot well deny;
And all I ask is a sunny day with the white clouds drifting,
And the engine's drone, the propeller's blur, and the
airfoils lifting.

And when at last I descend from the skies, from the pilot's
lofty life,
From the eagle's way and the lark's way where the wind's
like a whetted knife;
Then all I ask is to shoot the breeze with my grounded
fellow-flyers,
When the hangar doors are safely closed, and age has
quenched the fires.

Martin Barraclough
1936-

Because I Fly
Grover C Norwood

I have had no success in finding the author of this short piece of free verse which appears on several sites on the world-wide web and elsewhere. The title is the same as that of an excellent collection of aviation poetry, mostly American, edited by Helmut H Reda and published by McGraw-Hill in 2002.

Because I fly
I laugh more than other men
I look up and see more than they,
I know how the clouds feel,
What it's like to have the blue in my lap, to look down on
birds
To feel freedom in a thing called the stick...
Who but I can slice between God's billowed legs,
And feel the laugh and crash of his step
Who else has seen the unclimbed peaks?
The rainbow's secret?
The real reason birds sing?
Because I fly,
I envy no man on earth.

Grover C Norwood

Susie Coreth
(Author's photograph)

A Sonnet to the Sky
Susie Coreth, 15.6.2011

In response to my request to my pilot friends for their favourite aviation poetry, Susie, daughter of pilot and animal sculptor 'sans pareil', Mark Coreth, simply sat down and, before the day was out, had dashed off this priceless sonnet. No 'free verse' nonsense, the English sonnet has a strict discipline of 14 lines, 3 rhyming quartets ending with a couplet, 10 syllables per line and iambic pentameter – and all in an afternoon! Who says that artistic talent doesn't run in families?

Quiet all around, the wind has dropped,
A bird sings softly in the evening light,
A lingering smell of metal, dust and oil
Warmed from a day that had been shining bright.
I see it there, my little metal bird,
The sun seems caught upon it's glimmering tail,
It's waiting patiently for me to come,
Release it's breath; above the world to sail.
Suddenly the propeller starts to turn,
A wondrous sound across the valley heard,
We taxi, then the wheels lift off the ground,
I'm flying in my little metal bird.
And as I reach the pink and golden sky,
I think 'this is the life': to soar, to fly.

Susie Coreth
1991-

With talent such as this from young poets of today lovers of poetry can be optimistic that the continuing development of aviation in all its forms will be captured in poetic verse for future generations.

Requiescat

Introduction

It is a sad fact that death should be one of the greatest inspirations for poetry and poetic writing. It is accepted behaviour not to speak ill of the dead (unless he or she was a villain!) so the most laudable qualities of the deceased are remembered and, if written by a poet or Romantic, are beautifully and movingly conveyed to the reader. Obituaries, like eulogies at memorial services, frequently disclose events and characteristics of the deceased which were previously unknown. So often I have read an obituary or listened to a eulogy, wishing that I had been able to ask the late hero about his or her involvement in the aeronautical event being described. I have discovered, however, that heroes don't talk about such things, so it is left to the writer of the obituary and the orator to create the lasting record by which the late hero will best be remembered and by which the reader or listener will be inspired.

The beautiful memorial window placed in the church at Eastchurch to commemorate the late Hon. Charles S. Rolls and the late Mr. Cecil Grace.

(Flight)

In Memoriam – Cecil Grace
Dorothy M Haward

On 22nd December, 1910, a 30-year old American-born pioneer aviator, Cecil Grace, holder of Royal Aero Club Certificate No.4, took off from Swingate Downs in a Short pusher biplane in an attempt to win the Baron de Forest £4,000 prize for the longest flight from England into continental Europe. Thick sea mist and strong winds caused him to land in Calais and he decided to return to Eastchurch via Dover and to attempt the record on another day. He took off at ten past two in the afternoon and was expected over Dover in forty minutes, but by half past three had not arrived. The coastguard from Ramsgate sighted an aeroplane about six miles out to sea near the Goodwin Sands heading north. A few days later Grace's goggles and cap were washed ashore in Belgium.

Grace, who two months before his death had been naturalised as a British citizen, was posthumously awarded the Royal Aero Club's Gold Medal for his achievements as a pilot and an aviator. A stained glass window in All Saints' church, Eastchurch, on the Isle of Sheppey was jointly dedicated to him and Charles Rolls, the motoring and aviation pioneer. Rolls, with Henry Royce, founded Rolls-Royce and was the first Briton to be killed in a flying accident when the tail of his Wright Flyer broke off during a flying display near Bournemouth on 12th July, 1910.

He is lost! In the dusk of the evening
  The Goodwins have seen his last flight;
Then the mists hid his path, while around him
  Came stealing the arms of the night.
He is lost to the joy of the sunlight,
  The glory of life and its zest;
But he finds what the whole world is seeking –
  A well-honoured rest.

He is lost! When the feet of the morning
  Made rosy the slumbering sea,
The plane that she yesterday smiled on
  Had vanished for ever. And he –
He was lost to the world that laments him,
  And lost to the realms of the air;
But he finds the true source of all knowledge
  In kingdoms more fair.

He is lost! For the white planes that bore him
  So bravely have failed him, alas!
The sea is the grave that enclosed him,
  The winds sang his requiem Mass.
He is lost! And the hearts that have loved him
  Are weeping with longing and pain;
But we know, when all losing is over,
  We find him again.

He is lost! 'Mid the waste of the waters
  He sleeps, in the flower of his youth,
But we know when his spirit awakens
  It will be to the fullness of truth.
Feathered songsters spread swiftly your pinions,
  And there where the young hero lies,
Pay your homage to one who excelled you
  As lord of the skies.

Dorothy M Haward

Captain Guynemer
Florence Earle Coates

Georges Guynemer was born in Compiegne, France, in 1894. Despite being rejected for military service, he enlisted as a mechanic, and subsequently became one of France's top fighter aces in World War I. He flew with Escadrille N.3 (Storks) and was awarded the Legion d'Honneur, Croix de Guerre and Medaille Militaire. Guynemer was so successful that he was able to influence French fighter aircraft design. His *avion magique* was the Spad XII which, at his request, was armed with a 37 mm single-shot cannon firing through the propeller shaft – as well as a 7.62 mm machine gun. The cannon had to be manually re-loaded and every time it was fired had a heavy recoil and filled the cockpit with fumes – not an aircraft for the novice pilot; nevertheless Guynemer used it to good effect.

Guynemer failed to return from a mission on 11th September, 1917 and was reported as having been shot down by an overwhelming force of enemy fighters. His tally was 53 German aircraft and he himself survived being shot down seven times. A shy man, he was embarrassed by the lionization of the French Press. He was 22 when he died.

Florence Earle Coates was born in Philadelphia in 1850. She wrote six books of poetry and the lyrics for many songs. She strongly supported America's involvement in World War I, hence her interest in Guynemer's short but heroic life. Her credo was "The business of art is to enlarge and correct the heart and to lift our ideals out of the ugly and the mean through love of the ideal... The business of art is to appeal to the soul." Her poem was first printed in *A Treasury of War Poetry* in 1919.

Georges Guynemer, 1894-1917, by Lucien

Florence Earle Coates, 1850-1927

What high adventure, in what world afar,
Follows today,
Mid ampler air,
Heroic Guynemer?
What star,
Of all the myriad planets of our night,
Is by his glowing presence made more bright
Who chose the Dangerous way,
Scorning, while brave men died, ignobly safe to stay?

Into the unknown Vast,
Where few could follow him, he passed, –
On to the gate – the shadowy gate –
Of the Forbidden,
Seeking the knowledge jealous Fate
Had still so carefully from mortals hidden.

With vision falcon-keen,
His eyes beheld what others had not seen,
And his soul, with as clear a gaze,
Pierced through each clouded maze
Straight to the burning heart of things, and knew
The lying from the true.

A dweller in Immensity,
Of naught afraid,
He saw the havoc Tyranny had made, –
Saw the relentless tide of War's advance,
And high of heart and free,
Vowed his young life to Liberty –
And France!
O Compiegne! be proud of him – thy son, –
The greatest of the eagle brood, –
Who with intrepid soul the foe withstood,
And rests, his victories won!
Mourn not uncomforted, but rather say:

His wings were broken, but he led the way
Where myriad stronger wings shall follow;
For Wrong shall not hold lasting sway,
To break the World's heart, nor betray
With cruel pledges hollow!

To us the battle draweth near.
We dedicate ourselves again,
Remembering, O Compiegne!
Thy Charioteer –
Thy peerless one, who died to make men free,
And in Man's grateful heart shall live immortally!

Florence Earle Coates
1850-1927

In Memoriam – Sir Ross Smith
Shelbourne King, Frank McCabe

Sir Ross Smith, KBE, MC and Bar, DFC and Two Bars, AFC, was one of Australia's early pioneer aviators and air aces with 11 confirmed victories. A veteran of the Australian 3rd Light Horse and sometime pilot for Lawrence of Arabia, together with his brother, Sir Keith Smith, he made the first flight from London to Australia in 1919, in a Vickers Vimy. He was killed testing a Vickers Viking amphibian aircraft near Brooklands in 1922.

Both poems were sent from Australia by Sir Ross's mother, for inclusion in Stella Wolfe Murray's 1925 anthology, *The Poetry of Flight*.

Hast flown then on, O gallant heart,
  To worlds beyond our ken,
To live again a hero's part,
  Belov'd of gods and men?

Like eagle flying to the sun,
  Its brown wings bathed with light;
Earth's pangs forgotten, as if won
  The goal of its long flight.

To us the grey, to thee the gold
  Of sunset land today,
As softly to earth's quiet fold
  Thy body comes for aye.

But through the ages, Austral's son,
  Thy name will mean the praise
Of high endeavours, nobly won.
  And courage in all ways.

Shelbourne King

The WINNERS OF THE £10,000 PRIZE: the crew of the Vickers-Vimy-Rolls. From left to right: Sergt. W. H. Shiers, A.F.M., Lieut. K. M. Smith, R.A.F., Capt. Ross Smith, M.C., D.F.C., A.F.C., and Sergt. J. M. Bennett, M.S.M., A.F.M.

(Flight)

Sir Ross Smith's Vimy and crew for his record flight from London to Australia in 1919 *(Flight)*

And you are gone, Napoleon of the air,
Who swooped to home and fame in one great flight,
Who bridged the seas and dared the desert's death
Half a world crossed, and in the fight
'Gainst Nature's laws and man's indifference
With courage common to Australian youth, resource,
Bush-born, and faith unshakable
In man's power to do that of which he dreamed –
You faced the odds, and by the will to win,
Made hills of mountains, lakes of oceans vast;
Piloting your noble crew through trackless ways,
Till came the day this message thrilled the world –
"Ross Smith arrived!" A world's heart beat fast,
Another milestone in its march was passed.
Thus on the march of man towards things that were
But dreams, Australia played a part, and but for fate
Which whirls men and things around, and in its freaks,
Respects not even him his fellows may deem great,
She would have in her son gained further fame;
But fate has said, did not that deed of his
Place him among supermen? The work he planned,
Another brain and hand may execute. E'en were it done
It were no more than his... To this we bow
Yet softly falls the tear, we are but men, and
Childishly would claim him as our own, when
He was all the world's. And now his race is run
And mankind mourns a great and noble son.

Frank McCabe

Sir Charles Kingsford Smith, MC, AFC, 1897-1935

Kingsford Smith
Winifred Tennant

Winifred Coombe Tennant, born Winifred Pearce-Serocold in Gloucestershire, became a suffragette, and a fervent admirer of Lloyd George who appointed her delegate to the first assembly of the League of Nations. Although she never quite mastered the Welsh language she became a Welsh nationalist and 'Mistress of the Robes' in Gorsedd y Beird. She adopted many causes and also became a celebrated medium.

Why she should have written this eulogy to Sir Charles Kingsford Smith, MC, AFC, the great Australian pioneer pilot, is a mystery. 'Smithy', who was knighted for his many record flights, disappeared with his co-pilot, Tommy Petheridge, in his Lockheed Altair, *Lady Southern Cross*, on 8th November, 1935 while trying to beat the London to Australia speed record that was held by Scott and Campbell Black flying a de Havilland DH88 Comet. They were flying over the Indian Ocean at the time of their disappearance and, despite a huge search, no trace was ever found of the aircraft or their bodies.

Ask the sun; it has watched him pass –
A shadow mirrored on seas of glass;
Ask the stars that he knew so well
If they beheld where a bird-man fell.
Ask the wind that has blown with him
Over the edge of the ocean's rim,
Far from the charted haunts of men,
To the utmost limits and back again.
Ask the clouds on the mountain height,
The echoes that followed him in his flight,
The thunder that prowls the midnight sky,
If a silvered 'plane went riding by.
If the birds could talk, would they tell of the fall
Of a god who winged above them all?
Of an eagle-man, by the world's decrees,
King of the blue immensities?

Winifred Coombe Tennant
1874-1956

Gill Robb Wilson, 1892-1966

Amelia
Gill Robb Wilson

The world has an insatiable appetite for solving mysteries, particularly when they relate to famous people, and even today new efforts are being made to discover what really happened to Amelia Earhart when she disappeared over the Pacific in 1937.

Gill Robb Wilson wrote this tribute to her at the time of her disappearance in 1937.

Somewhere a fin on a lazy sea
And a broken prop on a coral key,
Somewhere a dawn whose morning star
Must etch dim light on a broken spar,
Somewhere a twilight that cannot go
Till it kisses the surf with afterglow;
But here, only silence and weary eyes
And an empty hangar and empty skies.

Somewhere the toss of a tousled head
In the secret of the angels overhead,
Somewhere a smile that would never fade
As the score reversed in the game she played,
Somewhere a spirit whose course held true
To do the thing that it wished to do;
But here, only silence and weary eyes
And an empty hangar and empty skies.

Gill Robb Wilson
1892-1966

Paul Day's sculpture of Battle of Britain pilots scrambling; part of the Battle of Britain Memorial on the Embankment, London

Untitled
J.L.P.

The Air Ministry issued weekly Casualty Communiques throughout the Second World War, listing hundreds of aircrew of the RAF, RAAF, RCAF, RNZAF and SAAF who were either 'killed in action', 'presumed killed in action', 'missing, believed killed in action', or just 'missing', along with copious corrections to earlier communiqués. All were printed each week in *Flight*. This poem, written on 10th June, 1940, at the beginning of the Battle of Britain, was positioned in the middle of the weekly Roll of Honour, Casualty Communique No. 240, printed in *Flight's* 10th June, 1943 issue.

He was too gay*, too young, to die;
So young he hardly knew the worth
Of England where he'd had his birth.
That England 'neath a cloud-flecked sky
For which he died: so to deny
The terror of the blackened hearth
The savage grins of Hun-like mirth.
He only knew the joy on high,
The blazing sun and racing cloud,
The hamlets of his peaceful land,
The plaudits of his people proud.
"A friendly soul and very grand"
This epitaph is but his shroud
For those, so few, who understand.

* In 1940 'gay' was still 'light-hearted and carefree'.

J.L.P.
10th June, 1940

In Memoriam – Timothy Corsellis Killed Flying
Patricia Ledward

Examples of Timothy Corsellis's poetry and a description of his short life are on pages 171-175 and 199. An ATA pilot, he was killed while ferrying a Miles Magister from White Waltham to Carlisle on 10th October, 1941.

Patricia Ledward was the daughter of sculptor, Gilbert Ledward, RA, OBE. She joined the ATS in 1942 and published poetry in many periodicals and anthologies. A year older than Corsellis, it is clear that they were close; both were poets – which would have strengthened that bond. Her powerful and moving poem is a fitting farewell to any war-time pilot-poet.

You wished to be a lark, and, as the lark, mount singing
To the highest peak of solitude your soul had found,
You wished to fly between the stars and let your song
Shower down to earth in gleaming falls of sound.

A century ago you might have done all this:
Flowers at your music would have set the earth on fire,
Mountains retained it in their hearts of rock,
In poplar boughs winds paused at your wild lyre.

World chaos coiled about you, and each upward flight
Meant struggling with the deep morass of history:
Luck was against you, poet, that you lived when guns
And tramping feet was all that mankind knew of poetry.

But solitude still called – you became an eagle.
Beneath your wings you held the slanting clouds of gold,
The earth seemed now a comic tune, for mighty orchestras
Drew you towards the sun, unblinded, bold.

A letter tells us you are dead – at twenty years.
From shocked and nerveless hands the paper slips.
We see it all – the failing engine, the numb fingers clutching,
The instantaneous fear, distorted lips,

The starting eyes, the whirling, humming sky,
The sweat of agony, the bleeding fist, the flash
Of life and panoramic view before your mind,
The whistling, screaming, downward rush, the crash.

The grass, the lonely hills, are weeping tears of green,
The sky bends low, embracing in a gentle shroud of air
Your shattered body; and the wind that sweeps the waves
Is mourning for your lively eyes and thick locks of your hair.

We, your friends, will not give way to alien tears,
But shall think in firelight of your grave voice reading verse,
Remember all your wit, your poses, and your heart
Far kinder than you'd ever have us guess.

Come! Let us dance in nightclubs you frequented,
Covet with envious eyes half-breeds you wished to gain,
Thrust our hands deep in golden hair you loved to touch,
Drink till your memory ferments within our brain.

The band is changing tune to the century's Blues:
Go on, yes, dance, I'll come when I am needed –
On a far hill a youth lies dead, his mouth towards the mud,
And, like the blood his song dissolves in earth, unheeded.

Play on, O Harlem band, O swing your blues!
Rend every stone with your terrible, lamenting cry:
Those who would sing of life, and hope, and joy,
Are driven out to hunt, to kill, to die.

Patricia Ledward
1920-

Crashed
Alexandra Etheldreda Grantham

Born in 1867, Alexandra Etheldreda Grantham was a poet of the First World War and a writer on Chinese history and art. One of her sons was killed at Gallipoli in June, 1915 and another son, Pilot Officer Godfrey Grantham, who flew with the Royal Air Force Volunteer Reserve (RAFVR), was killed on 21st June, 1942.

An hour ago or less this piteous tangled heap
Made up of metal bits whose scattered fragments show
Black trace of flames attacking it with deadly leap
An hour ago.

Soared in the blue, triumphant like a star, sheer glow
Of silver on great wings spread wide in spirals steep
To rise and climb o'er midnight clouds of ice and snow,

And he who swept it upwards – slain, never to reap
The harvest of his dreams, nor wondrous joys to know
Of coming home, nor wake again. He laughed at sleep
An hour ago.

Alexandra Etheldreda Grantham

IM – Richard Hillary, RAFVR
Wrenne Jarman

Flying a Spitfire over the North Sea during the Battle of Britain at the age of twenty-one, Flight Lieutenant Richard Hillary was shot down and badly burned. He was sent to Queen Victoria Hospital, East Grinstead, Sussex where his face and hands were re-built over many months by Archibald McIndoe, the pioneer in plastic surgery. Hillary was sent on a tour of the United States giving lectures for the Ministry of Information, and while there he wrote his book, *The Last Enemy*, a classic of its time and subject. One description of a pilot is timeless.

"It is only in the air that a pilot can grasp that feeling, that flash of knowledge, of insight, that matures him beyond his years; only in the air that he knows suddenly he is a man in a world of men. 'Coming back to earth' has for him a double significance. He finds it difficult to orientate himself in a world that is so worldly, amongst a people whose conversation seems to him brilliant, minds agile, and knowledge complete – yet a people somehow blind. It is very strange."

Hillary eventually bullied his way back to flying duties with an Operational Training Unit in Berwickshire. He died in an air accident on 8th January, 1943, aged twenty-three.

Dazed, with the trumpets sounding in his ears,
He felt, reluctantly, Life's staying hand:
Saw fade the splendour of the ardent years,
And waited what, so late, life should command.
Mute morning shadows mocked him while he slept
Within his broken manhood – as a spark
Glowed, flickered, paled to ash again, and crept
Back from the day into forgetting dark.

From 'The Last Enemy' by Richard Hillary, published by Pimlico

(Used by permission of The Random House Group Limited)

But resolution paced beside his pain
And love brought light again to quenched young eyes,
And tongues of courage lit and leapt again,
Arching like rainbows over shaken skies.
Sunlight moved on him – and then in him
Memory of flight in windy caverns of air:
The lift of eagle, soar of seraphim,
And fields where only he and planets were.

Steeled and remote, the grafted man arose
And knew he must inhabit once again
The lucent realm that had been his, espouse
Anew the bride that had desired his pain.
This time, the high exacting gods approved
His gift made perfect in the passioned clay,
And took the clean oblation, which they loved…
And Life was dumb, and turned her head away.

He had known evil; seen the vampire Thing,
Waxed swollen on the treason in man's heart,
Stronger than man, than nation, battening, –

But from the moral clinch he was apart:
He has no politics who only draws
A shining pattern on the startled night
In careless glory, like a meteor's
Ardent signature in lovely light.

Wrenne Jarman
1905-1953

Group Captain Percy Charles Pickard DSO**, DFC, RAF, 1915-1944

Target Amiens
(IM Group Captain Pickard, RAF)
Wrenne Jarman

On 18th February, 1944, Group Captain Percy Charles (Pick) Pickard, aged 28, and already holder of three DSOs and the DFC, led a special force of eighteen Mosquitos in a low-level daylight attack on Amiens prison where, it was reported, members of the French Resistance were about to be executed. Code-named *Operation Jericho*, the controversial raid was a success and the walls of the prison were breached to allow members of the Maquis to escape. Although there was great loss of life among the inmates, 258 of them got away. Tragically Pickard and his navigator, Flight Lieutenant "Bill" Broadley, DSO, DFC, DFM, were both killed when their Mosquito was shot down in the closing stages of the raid.

To this day it is not publically known who authorised this raid and for what real purpose.

Grey walls shadowed, grey walls star-lit,
Taut at the end of the white road's rope
Men that the dawn would etch in scarlet,
Breathless for death in the graveyard of hope.

Fighters' swift weaving, over and under,
Smooth loads falling like drops from a knife,
Stone walls tearing like paper asunder,
Black mites racing for thickets and life.

Odyssey over, soaring to skyward,
Nosing to north and the wind from the sea –
Left behind, for a toast and a byword,
Hearts grown great in the old chivalry.

Wrenne Jarman
1905-1953

Returned Airman
Pauline Lendon

Pauline Lendon served in the Womens' Auxiliary Air Force (WAAF) during the war. The Waafs, as they were known, did many essential jobs on RAF airfields and much to keep up the morale of aircrew.

One of their hardest jobs, however, was to help tend wounded and dying men lifted from aircraft which returned, badly damaged, after a bombing raid. This heart-rending poem from Anne Powell's *Shadows of War* is a small example of the courage and compassion shown by those brave women.

Die peacefully brave boy I do not know
O God please hear my prayer and help you now
Morphia calms the pain of but a while ago
And smooths the fear wracked furrows from your brow

The morning star that lately was your guide
That served in place of navigator lost
Is waiting now for you in humble pride
Who saved friends' lives and didn't count the cost

Your blood that stains my battle-dress grows chill
The flames light up the pallor of your lips
Your breath comes fainter pulse is almost still
The hand that clasps my own goes limp and slips

Die peacefully young hero yet unnamed
Neath fading bomber's moon on grass dew wet
We who remain may live to feel ashamed
But even so we never can forget

Pauline Lendon
1924-

Death of a Prince
Bernard Chabbert

Bernard Chabbert wrote *Letter from France* for *PILOT* magazine during the last two decades of the 20th century. His written English was impeccable, which he attributed wholeheartedly to his journalistic mentor, the owner and editor of *PILOT*, James Gilbert. Bernard was a very close friend of the Hannas and felt deeply the tragic death of Mark at the age of forty, and the awful vacuum it left in his father Ray's life. These attributes, combined with Gallic emotion, produced one of the most deeply moving obituaries I have ever read, and one whose sentiments are timeless.

When Mark Hanna died in a Barcelona hospital, his father Ray by his side, we lost – and I choose my words with care – we lost a prince of the skies.

After such an event, pilots revert to tradition and immerse themselves in whys and hows, to avoid staring directly into the void. So now, one of the questions is: why did that Messerschmitt slash into the ground, as it did? Mark had made a low and fast tailwind fly-by over the runway. Zooming above the threshold into a 4g pull-up into the down-wind leg, everything seemed to go according to the book, gear down, flaps down, radiators open, prop forward... Why, after swooping into a graceful, low-power approach and curving the brutish-looking fighter to the very end of the short run-way, did he fall into a vertical bank and stay there until the ground caught the wingtip? One of those who witnessed it said, "I suddenly had the strange feeling of watching a pilotless aircraft falling inexorably to the ground..."

Ray has since told me that one possibility being examined was that, on that windless afternoon, Mark may have flown into his own high-energy wingtip vortices, still active and slowly drifting across finals, then found himself rolled into a high-bank position

Mark Hanna, on the wing of the OFMC's P-51, 'Big Beautiful Doll', with the author's sons in the cockpit. Le Touquet, 1996.
(Author's photograph)

from where he was unable to recover. Opening up would not have helped – propeller torque would only have aggravated the bank.

Mark Hanna was a magnificent person. The ladies were devastated by his looks, and men wanted to be among his friends. He was one of the most courteous people in the world, and had a particular gift of putting everyone around at ease. Talking with Mark, you felt brilliant, wise, generous, because he was all that, and more.

Mark's life revolved around one strong concept: he had respect for the world around him. He respected other people, their opinions and their work. He respected the natural law, and nature's laws, especially physics, because physics governs flight and because flight ran through him, like blood. He was a realist, but he recognised the line between realism and cynicism. He always kept his feet firmly planted on solid ground. Mark was the son every father dreams of, and he had the father of every son's dreams. He did not call Ray "Dad", but simply "Father". In today's world, a son who uses that word and puts so much respect and affection into it is a precious man indeed.

We had a great time at La Roche-sur-Yon, during the airshow there last summer, for Mark's fortieth birthday. The airshow was organised by Michel Dubreuil's sons and family, to commemorate Michel's death in his P-51 just a year before. Strange that. Marking this close friend and fine man's demise turned into a real celebration of life, and the love of it, and Mark, despite being bone-tired, had his laughs. At forty years old you are not a kid anymore, nor a young man. At forty, Mark was more handsome than ever, and women as well as men had to acknowledge that he represented a kind of human perfection.

His flying bordered on the miraculous. He was majestic in the way he manoeuvred in the air, taking possession of the sky, neither forcing his machine nor pushing the laws of aerodynamics. In his hands any aircraft could be made to dance.

His life, seen from the outside, had a dreamlike, almost movie star quality. But the truth was that being Mark Hanna was not that easy. One day, some time after having resigned from the RAF and joined the Old Flying Machine Company full-time, he had told me, "I have no money, no house of my own, not even my own car, no woman can possibly put up with my life-style for long, but I can fly a Spitfire up and around the clouds whenever I want to... I suppose it's a price I have to pay!"

Mark's real trade was flying fighters. Being Ray Hanna's son had made things rougher when he joined the RAF; Ray had left his mark across the Service, if only because of the flamboyant way he led the Red Arrows. In my opinion Ray is one of the five best airmen who ever flew, full stop. Growing up as his aviator son, then, was a full-size problem. But Mark worked out solutions, and soon was known as 'the other Hanna'. He became a brilliant Phantom pilot, and such was his affinity for that monster of an aircraft, when he was offered a transfer to the fly-by-wire Tornado he said, "Thanks, but no thanks," putting his military career in jeopardy. Instead, he opted for romantic aviation, and took charge of the OFMC, joining his father to create one of the outstanding teams in the history of aeronautics.

His first big airshow was at La Ferte-Alais, a long time ago. The day before the show, Ray and Mark arrived late in the afternoon in P-40 and Spitfire – their famous MH434. Ray had landed the P-40 trailing smoke: it turned out an electrical fire was busy consuming the fuel pump mounted inside the fuselage, behind the cockpit.

After the electrical fire had been put out, father and son went to work. Ray wanted Mark to rehearse his sequence. It was a balmy early May evening. The grass field was silent, but for birdsong in the woods. Ray was standing on the Spitfire wing, beside the cockpit, preparing his son for his first public demo. Ray was murmuring advice, Mark's eyes were focused on infinity. Their conference lasted for ten full minutes, Mark sometimes shaking his leather-helmeted head, sometimes nodding. I was watching them from a distance, and I knew that this was not so much instructor-to-student chat, as the transfer of pure art between an established virtuoso and his heir.

Then Mark fired up the Merlin and, within five minutes, he was stretching the aircraft into a trajectory just like a musician shapes his notes. Then he landed, the prop flicked to a halt, and Ray jumped up on the wing. For the next ten minutes they debriefed. Twenty minutes of talk for just five minutes in the air.

Now it's over, and I have difficulty in accepting it. I look back at all these years filled with aerial jubilation, and I see too many fading faces. I have a feeling that, within that small world of romantic aviation, dead friends now outnumber living brothers. Some of them were just chaps, some took charge of my initiation like Hoof Proudfoot when he took me into that strange heavenly territory up there the day we flew a Spitfire. Some like Pierre Dague were true brothers. Ray, Mark and I were working on future plans...

A few months ago Ray had said to me, "I am thinking of putting an end to professional display flying. I'd like to go back home to New Zealand with two or three aircraft and enjoy free flying across blue skies, oceans and mountains. I'm getting a bit old you know..."

Mark had told me, a few years ago, "Father is a living miracle. I watch for any sign of degradation in the way he flies. There is none. When we play air combat together, he always beats me..."

Now Mark is gone, and my thoughts turn to Ray.

Bernard Chabbert
1944-

Ray Hanna continued display flying Spitfire MH434 until 2005 when he died of natural causes at the age of 77.

James Gilbert, editor and publisher of *Pilot* for nearly thirty years, died on 14 February 2006.

(From Pilot, April 2006, by kind permission of the Editor)

James Gilbert
Maxi Gainza

A regular contributor to *PILOT* magazine while under the ownership and editorship of James Gilbert, Argentinian Maxi Gainza's writings belie his origins. When his family was banished from Argentina to Uruguay he, as a small boy of 5, was sent to the British School of Montevideo where speaking English was compulsory under threat of punishment. He later studied English as an undergraduate at Kings College, London and polished off his linguistic and writing skills with a post-graduate degree in Arturian Literature at Oxford. His flight reports of front-line military aircraft were beautifully written, his descriptive powers and romantic approach to the business of flying 'heavy metal' setting the standard for such reports during the last twenty-five years. Like Bernard Chabbert, Maxi attributes his journalistic success to the mentorship of James Gilbert.

This tribute to James, together with many others, appeared in the April 2006 issue of *PILOT*.

I first met James thirty-four years ago, in the air. I was heading back to Redhill and he departing from it and coming my way. I recognised his Bucker Jungmeister by how he had described it in his book *The Great Planes* with its 'tiny balloon wheels on that ridiculous, forward-jutting undercarriage (that) seemed to reach down for the earth like the paws of a jumping cat'.

Fresh from reading that enthralling aviation masterpiece, it now seemed as if James and his fabled machine had sprung out of its pages. As we crossed I couldn't resist turning hard in behind him, wondering if the word-meister could fly as well as he wrote – believing my Zlin 526 to have the edge over his draggier mount.

He obviously saw it coming, for he pulled up and in no time reappeared glued to my tail. Try as I desperately did, I couldn't shake him off. When I finally gave up and resumed a steady course, he drew up alongside, stared quizzically through his large prescription glasses, and smiled.

That smile of his, warm and game, had a soothing effect on my bruised pilot's ego, and like the Cheshire Cat's in Alice in Wonderland, it lingered long after he'd peeled off and vanished in the evening sky.

It still does now, tempering the loss of a friend who not only believed I could write in what to me is a second language, but who also taught me by example never to take myself, or anyone else, too seriously. Not even terminal illness, which I saw him endure with stoical equanimity and sense of humour, deflected him from this life-long desideratum.

James revelled in challenging authority in its many guises and in deflating vanities. I remember him once at a Farnborough Air Show cutting in mid-flow a glib Airbus official vaunting the market competitiveness of their latest product: "Indeed, on tax-payers' money," he quipped. Still, his happiest moments were next to his wife Gena and his children Alexander, Sophie, Max and Daisy, to whom my heart goes out as they now face life without grumpy but loving and infinitely caring James.

Surprisingly – or then, perhaps not – James and I never flew together. What we did a lot was meet for lunch at Alvaro's London restaurant 'La Famiglia' to discuss books – he was immensely well read – and express our shared love of flying like someone once said of poetry: as emotion recollected in tranquillity. We'd also catch up on members of the virtual family we all joined the day we got ourselves airborne of our own free will and turned the sky into our second nursery.

He is somewhere behind its blue curtains, watching over us, I trust.

Maxi Gainza
1949-

Tribute (to Sir Winston Churchill)

Avril Anderson

I must confess to stretching the parameters of this anthology in order to include this tribute.

In 1912, while First Lord of the Admiralty, Winston Churchill was responsible for the formation of the Royal Naval Air Service and the Air Department of the Admiralty. That same year he started taking flying lessons, sometimes making as many as ten flights in a day. After the deaths of his instructor in 1913 and Gustav Hamel in 1914, his family persuaded him to stop, but he took it up again after the Great War. On 18th July, 1919 he suffered a crash on take-off with his instructor, the ex-Commandant of the Central Flying School, Colonel Alan Scott, MC, who had himself broken both legs while learning to fly. Winston was shaken and badly bruised, but it proved to be too much for his wife, Clementine, and he was persuaded to give up. He never went solo, but for the rest of his life retained great enthusiasm for aviation and often took the controls of the aeroplane in which he was flying.

During the Second World War, as Honorary Air Commodore of 615 Squadron, he often wore Air Commodore's uniform, his many military decorations being surmounted by RAF pilot's wings, which he proudly wore as the sole recipient of the honorary award of this brevet.

On 30th January, 1965, with thousands of others I stood on Ludgate Hill to watch the funeral procession of the great man as it made its way to St. Paul's Cathedral. On television Richard Dimbleby read this tribute by Avril Anderson at the end of Sir Winston's funeral.

Sir Winston after taking a flying lesson in a BE2C (Renault engine) in 1912

(Reproduced with permission of Curtis Brown, London, on behalf of the Broadwater Collection and Churchill Archives Centre. BRDW 1 Photo 2/49)

Sir Winston at the controls of BOAC Boeing 314 Flying Boat en route from Virginia to Bermuda, January 16th, 1942

(Imperial War Museum Catalog H16645)

From the Hall of Kings they bore him then,
The greatest of all Englishmen,
To the Nation's, the World's, Requiem
At Bladon.

Drop, English Earth, on him beneath,
To our sons and their sons, bequeath
His glories, and our pride and grief
At Bladon.

For lion heart that lies below
That feared not toil, nor tears, nor foe,
Let the oak stand, though tempests blow
At Bladon.

So Churchill sleeps; yet surely wakes,
Old warrior, where the morning breaks
On sunlit uplands, – but the heart aches
At Bladon.

Avril Anderson

Requiem Hymn for an Airman
Martin Barraclough

I was originally inspired to write this hymn on the death of Sir Thomas Sopwith in February 1989, but worked on it for the next six years, making various improvements, so that, among other things, it would (as my friend Juliet Grasby insisted) conform to the dactylic measure of the music.

I have waived all copyright so that anyone is welcome to use it.

Sing to the music of St. Clement (Hymn 477 A&M)

My wings, O Father, Thou hast folded
But grant I pray this last request
That I may spread them once more only
And fly to heaven's eternal rest.

I can no longer hear the engines
That powered me upwards to the sky
Beside Thy power, Great Lord, they falter
Thy power is constant, ever nigh.

If Man should fly, Dear Lord, for ever
Then fly beside him night and day
To make Thy purpose his endeavour
And bring him safely down I pray.

Although my night now falls for ever
There surely dawn in the eastern sky
Bright days for flights of hope and mercy
To serve Thy holy will on high.

So take me, God, on this last journey
And bear me up on wings sublime
Make peace on earth Thy lasting glory
And peace in the air our cause divine.

If the "Amen" is to be sung, it should be on a single note, starting quietly, building up to a crescendo and then tailing off into silence – as if a fast jet had flown overhead from one horizon and disappeared over the opposite horizon.

Martin Barraclough
1936-

Finis

Introduction

I end this anthology with two haunting poems.

The first is Maurice Baring's *In Memoriam – AH*. Maurice was the eighth child and fifth son of Edward Baring, first Baron Revelstoke, of the banking family. He was a man of letters who joined the Royal Flying Corps at the age of forty and served in France as 'mentor and guide' to Hugh Trenchard, father of the Royal Air Force. Trenchard said of him, "He was the most unselfish man I have ever met or am likely to meet. The Flying Corps owed to this man much more than they know or think."

The artist Sir William Orpen wrote that Baring's *In Memoriam*, written in memory of his close friend, Auberon Herbert, Captain Lord Lucas, RFC, was "the greatest work of art that's come out of this whole war".

Herbert was a true countryman and went to South Africa as war correspondent for the Times. The mismanagement of a bullet wound in the foot caused the loss of his leg but this did not stop him from pursuing all his old activities. Entering politics he ended up as President of the Board of Agriculture and at the age of forty, many years over age, he joined the Royal Flying Corps where he became a most competent pilot, 'his wonderful eye and nerve standing him in good stead'. Refusing command of a Squadron until he had served on the Western front, on 3rd November, 1916, he went missing on a flight over the German lines. His grave was found when British troops advanced to victory in 1918.

Maurice Baring himself began to suffer from Parkinson's Disease in the early 1930s but continued to write. He was ultimately looked after by friends and died unmarried at Beaufort Castle near Inverness in 1945.

The poem is as fine a tribute to a very dear lost friend as you will ever find.

The second poem is by the great American pilot poet Gill Robb Wilson and is called *To Find Myself*. It must strike a chord with all pilots, whatever stage of their flying career they have reached, but particularly with those who face a life that no longer has wings.

In Memoriam, A H
Maurice Baring

The wind has blown away the rain
That all day long had soaked the level plain.
Against the horizon's fiery rack,
The sheds loomed black.
And higher, in their tumultuous concourses met,
The streaming clouds, shot-riddled banners, wet
With the flickering storm
Drifted and smouldered, warm
With flashes sent
From the lower firmament.
And they concealed –
They only here and there through rifts revealed
A hidden sanctuary of fire and light,
A city of chrysolite.

We looked and laughed and wondered, and I said:
That orange sea, those oriflammes outspread
Were like the fanciful imaginings
That the young painter flings
Upon the canvas bold,
Such as the sage and the old
Make mock at, saying that it could never be;
And you assented also, laughingly.
I wondered what they meant,
That flaming firmament,
Those clouds so grey so gold, so wet so warm,
So much of glory and so much of storm,
The end of the world, or the end
Of the war – remoter still to me and you, my friend.

Alas! it meant not this, it meant not that:
It meant that now the last time you and I
Should look at the golden sky,
And the dark fields large and flat,
And smell the evening weather,
And laugh and talk and wonder both together.

The last, last time. We nevermore should meet
In France or London street,
Or fields of home. The desolated space
Of life shall nevermore
Be what it was before.
No one shall take your place.
No other face
Can fill that empty frame.
There is no answer when we call your name.
We cannot hear your step upon the stair.
We turn to speak and find a vacant chair.
Something is broken which we cannot mend.
God has done more than take away a friend
In taking you; for all that we have left
Is bruised and irremediably bereft.
There is none like you. Yet not that alone
Do we bemoan;
But this; that you were greater than the rest,
And better than the best.

O liberal heart fast-rooted to the soil,
O lover of ancient freedom and proud toil,
Friend of the gipsies and all wandering song,
The forest's nurseling and the favoured child
Of woodlands wild –
O brother to the birds and all things free,
Captain of liberty!
Deep in your heart the restless seed was sown;
The vagrant spirit fretted in your feet;
We wondered could you tarry long,

And brook for long the cramping street,
Or would you one day sail for shores unknown,
And shake from you the dust of towns, and spurn
The crowded market-place – and not return?
You found a sterner guide;
You heard the guns. Then, to their distant fire,
Your dreams were laid aside;
And on that day, you cast your heart's desire
Upon a burning pyre;
You gave your service to the exalted need,
Until at last from bondage freed,
At liberty to serve as you loved best,
You chose the noblest way. God did the rest.

So when the spring of the world shall shrive our stain,
After the winter of the war,
When the poor world awakes to peace once more,
After such night of ravage and of rain,
You shall not come again.
You shall not come to taste the old spring weather,
To gallop through the soft untrampled heather,
To bathe and bake your body on the grass.
We shall be there, alas!
But not with you. When Spring shall wake the earth,
And quicken the scarred fields to the new birth,
Our grief shall grow. For what can Spring renew
More fiercely for us than the need of you?

That night I dreamt they sent for me and said
That you were missing. 'Missing, missing – dead':
I cried when in the morning I awoke,
And all the world seemed shrouded in a cloak;
But when I saw the sun,
And knew another day had just begun,
I brushed the dream away, and quite forgot
The nightmare's ugly blot.
So was the dream forgot. The dream came true.

Before the night I knew
That you had flown away into the air
For ever. Then I cheated my despair.
I said
That you were safe – or wounded – but not dead.
Alas! I knew
Which was the false and true.
And after days of watching, days of lead,
There came the certain news that you were dead.
You had died fighting, fighting against odds,
Such as in war the gods
Aethereal dared when all the world was young;
Such fighting as blind Homer never sung,
Nor Hector nor Achilles never knew;
High in the empty blue.
High, high, above the clouds, against the setting sun,
The fight was fought, and your great task was done.

Of all your brave adventures this the last
The bravest was and best;
Meet ending to a long embattled past,
This swift, triumphant, fatal quest,
Crowned with the wreath that never perisheth,
And diadem of honourable death;
Swift Death aflame with offering supreme
And mighty sacrifice,
More than all mortal dream;
A soaring death, and near to Heaven's gate;
Beneath the very walls of Paradise.
Surely with soul elate,
You heard the destined bullet as you flew,
And surely your prophetic spirit knew
That you had well deserved that shining fate.

Here is no waste,
No burning Might-have-been,
No bitter after-taste,
None to censure, none to screen,
Nothing awry, nor anything misspent;
Only content, content beyond content,
Which hath not any room for betterment.

God, Who made you valiant, strong and swift,
And maimed you with a bullet long ago,
And cleft your riotous ardour with a rift,
And checked your youth's tumultuous overflow,
God gave back your youth to you,
And packed in moments rare and few
Achievements manifold
And happiness untold,
And bade you spring to Death as to a bride,
In manhood's ripeness, power and pride,
And on your sandals strong wings of youth.
He let you leave a name
To shine on the entablatures of truth,
For ever:
To sound for ever in answering halls of fame.

For you soared onwards to that world which rags
Of clouds, like tattered flags,
Concealed; you reached the walls of Chrysolite,
The mansions white;
And losing all, you gained the civic crown
Of that eternal town,
Wherein you passed a rightful citizen
Of that bright commonwealth beyond our ken.

Surely you found companions meet for you
In that high place;
You met there face to face
Those you had never known, but whom you knew;
Knights of the Table Round,
And all the very brave, the very true,
With chivalry crowned;
The captains rare,
Courteous and brave beyond our human air;
Those who had loved and suffered overmuch,
Now free from the world's touch.
And with them were the friends of yesterday,
Who went before and pointed you the way;
And in that place of freshness, light and rest,
Where Lancelot and Tristram vigil keep
Over their King's long sleep,
Surely they made a place for you,
Their long-expected guest,
Among the chosen few,
And welcomed you, their brother and their friend,
To that companionship which hath no end.
And in the portals of the sacred hall
You hear the trumpet's call,
At dawn upon the silvery battlement,
Re-echo through the deep
And bid the sons of God to rise from sleep,
And with a shout to hail
The sunrise on the city of the Grail:
The music that proud Lucifer in Hell
Missed more than all the joys that he forwent.
You hear the solemn bell

At vespers, when the oriflammes are furled;
And then you know that somewhere in the world,
That shines far-off beneath you like a gem,
They think of you, and when you think of them
You know that they will wipe away their tears,
And cast aside their fears;
That they will have it so,
And in no otherwise;
That it is well with them because they know,
With faithful eyes,
Fixed forward and turned upwards to the skies,
That it is well with you,
Among the chosen few,
Among the very brave, the very true.

Wing Commander Maurice Baring, OBE, RAF
1874-1945

To Find Myself
Gill Robb Wilson

When the time comes that you look
back down the trail in nostalgic wonder,
remembering the accumulated hours and
the far places and the almost forgotten ships
you have flown – when you recall the
judgements and decisions, some right and some
fearfully wrong – when you relive the
accented moments of exhilaration
and breathcatching awe or the mingled ones
of hope and despair – when word for word
there comes to mind accompanied by
the dull chatter of long-silent guns
some muttered snatch of prayer –
then you must ask yourself as have I –
what did I seek that I had to find in the sky?

What did I have to know that made me
lift with hammering heart and uncertain skill
against the thermal tides – what beyond
the written page to learn besides –
whom did I hope to meet and make my friend
in the vast solitudes of space –
what was there to be had that I must claim
from the distant market place –
and, if the sights and sounds and smells of all
the earth around remained beyond my ken
and wondrous names conjured no memories to my
mind, what were the odds –
was life not pleasant on the land and sea
that I should seek the sky –
what did I have to find that I should fly?

Not that I have a pride in what I found
or that some find less in nearer scenes and
more familiar plans – but for me
the skies were the promised lands and I had
to know how a heart must hush to hear
the voice from the burning bush –
and I had to know what the mountain said when
a humble man bowed down his head –
and I had to go where the giants dwelt to see
how a man with a slingshot felt –
and I had to lift my timid soul to learn
if the clod comprised the whole –
and now I know what I sought to find that
made me walk with the sun and wind –
it was myself, myself.

Gill Robb Wilson
1892-1966

Acknowledgements

I must first thank my constant guide and mentor, Tony Gray, of WORDS BY DESIGN, who has created this and all my earlier books out of pages of enthusiastic scribbling.

I am immensely grateful to Murdo Morrison, editor of *Flight Global*, for his kind permission to reproduce both written material and illustrations from the many volumes of *Flight* between 1909 and 1960 which I was fortunate to purchase at auction in 1987. As well as providing some early poetry they have been an unfailing source of contemporary photographs.

Special thanks are also due to Tim Pierce, Assistant Librarian at the Royal Air Force College, Cranwell, for allowing me access to the college library and their collection of aviation poetry and photographs.

The world-wide web and Google have been an invaluable source of information.

All acknowledgements of illustrations appear below the picture concerned.

I also gratefully acknowledge the following for their permission to print certain poems and to reproduce copyright material.

Alan Brodie Representation Ltd., (www.alanbrodie.com) representative of NC Aventales AG 1944, Successor in title to the estate of Noel Coward, for *Lie In The Dark And Listen*.

A.P.Watt Ltd., first, on behalf of The Trustees of the Maurice Baring Will Trust for *In Memoriam A.H.* by Maurice Baring, from *Poems, 1914-1916*, published by Martin Secker, 1920; and secondly, on behalf of Timothy d'Arch Smith for *Eyes in the Air* from *The Guns*, by Gilbert Frankau, published by Chatto and Windus in 1916.

Cambridge University Press, for permission to use In Memoriam (*Timothy Corsellis, killed flying*), by Patricia Ledward, from *Poems of This War By Younger Poets*, edited by Patricia Ledward and Colin Strang, published in 1942. © Cambridge University Press.

Chabbert, Bernard, for his obituary of Mark Hanna from *PILOT*, February, 2000.

Coreth, Susie, for her poem *A Sonnet to the Sky*, specially written for this anthology.

Corsellis, John, for his brother Timothy's poems, *The RAF*, *What I Never Saw*, *Coldly Land Slipped Away* and *Engine Failure*.

David Higham Associates, for John Pudney's poems, *For Johnny*, *Security*, *Combat Report* and *Air Gunner*, from *For Johnny*, published by Sheapherd Walwyn, 1976.

Douglas Hamilton, Diarmaid and Iain, for the poems *Flight*, *On Looking into a Pilot's Operational Log-book*, *Operational Log-book* and *New England* by their mother, Prunella Power.

Fleet Air Arm Officers Association for *The Stringbag Song*.

Foxley-Norris, Lady, for her late husband's poem *Envoi- Battle of Britain Pilot*.

Gainza, Maxi, for his obituary of James Gilbert from *PILOT*, April, 2006.

Grealy, Audrey, for her poems *Battle of Britain Pilot*, *The Price – 1940*, *Lancasters* and *Bomber County*.

Morgan, David, for his poems *Der Traum* and *Thoughts of Home*.

Norman, Sir Torquil, for the poems *For the Fly-leaf of an Anthology*, *Hamel's Departure*, *Hamel's Death*, *First Solo* and *Fighter Boy* by his father, Sir Nigel Norman.

Peters Fraser & Dunlop (www.petersfraserdunlop.com) on behalf of the estate of Cecil Day-Lewis, for *Battle of Britain* and *RAF – The Ancestors*, by Cecil Day-Lewis from *Overtures to Death* © Cecil Day Lewis.

Rae, Ian, for his poems *Flying Accident*, *Nuisance Raid* and *An Old Airfield* from *A Pilot's Notes* published by Woodfield Publishing Ltd, 2011.

Random House, Inc for permission to use *One of the Trusted* and *To Find Myself*, from *The Airman's World* by Gill Robb Wilson, ©1957 by Gill Robb Wilson. Copyright renewed 1985 by Mrs. George Denison.

Smith, Timothy d'Arch, for his Aunt Pamela's poem, *London – New York*.

Soames, Mary, for *The Bombers* by Sarah Churchill.

This England Publishing Ltd., for the poems *High Flight, Oh, Once Again* and *Per Ardua*, by John Magee from *John Magee, The Pilot Poet*, 1996.

Every effort has been made to trace all copyright holders and I apologise to anyone who inadvertently has not been acknowledged.

Bibliography

A Pilot's Notes, Poems of a World War Two Flying Instructor, by Ian Rae, published by Woodfield Publishing Ltd, 2011

Aeroplane Monthly, 1982-2011.

Because of These – Verses of the Royal Air Force, by Anthony Richardson, published by Hodder & Stoughton, 1942.

Flight, Volumes 1 to 60, 1909 to 1966.

Hostile Skies, by David Morgan, published by Orion Books Ltd, 2006.

John Magee, The Pilot Poet, published by This England Books, 1996

Men of the R.A.F. published by Oxford University Press, 1942

Pilot magazine, 1971-2011.

Poems, 1914-1919, by Maurice Baring, published by Martin Secker, 1920.

Poems and Rhymes, by Jeffery Day, published by Sidgwick and Jackson Ltd., 1919.

Spirit of Flight, compiled by Ian Gentle, published by NMS Publishing Ltd., 1999.

The Airman's World, by Gill Robb Wilson, published by Random House, New York, 1957.

The Complete Poems of C Day-Lewis, published by Stanford University Press, 1992.

The Dawn Patrol, and Other Poems of an Aviator, by Paul Bewsher, published by Erskine Macdonald Ltd., 1917.

The Fleet Air Arm Songbook, published by The Fleet Air Arm Officers Association.

The Last Enemy, by Richard Hillary, published by Pimlico, 1992.

The Unassuming Sky, Collected Poems 1938 – 1941, by Timothy Corsellis, chosen and presented by John Corsellis and Dr, Helen Goethals, to be published.

Verses 1911-1943, by Nigel Norman, published privately in 1999.

Verses of a Fighter Pilot, by Flying Officer A.N.C. Weir, DFC, published by Faber and Faber, 1941.

Wings of the Morning, by Ian Cameron, published by Hodder & Stoughton, 1962.

ANTHOLOGIES

Because I Fly, by Helmut H. Reda, published by Mcgraw Hill, 2002.

Icarus: An Anthology of the Poetry of Flight, by R. de la Bere, published by Macmillan & Co., 1939.

More Poems of the Second World War - the Oasis selection, published by J M Dent and Sons, 1989.

Shadows of War, by Anne Powell, published by Sutton Publishing Limited, 1999.

The Crowded Sky, by Neville Duke and Edward Lanchbery, published by Cassell & Company Ltd, 1959.

The Greenwood Anthology of New Verse, by Herbert Palmer, published by Frederick Muller, 1948.

The Muse in Arms, by E B Osborne, published by Murray, London, 1917.

The Poems We Wrote, An Anthology of Air Force Poems, by Eddy A. Coward, published by E.A. Coward, 1997.

The Poetry of Flight, An Anthology, by Stella Wolfe Murray, published by Heath Cranton Ltd, 1925.

The Voice of War, Poems of the Second World War, The Oasis Collection, published by Michael Joseph,1995.

War Poems from The Sunday Times, printed for private circulation,1945.

Wings: an Anthology of Flight by H.O. Bryden, published by Faber and Faber, 1942.

Index of Titles

R

S

T

Index of First Lines

Index of Authors

Give Me the WIngs